TU WAN'S
STONE CATALOGUE
OF CLOUDY FOREST

A Commentary and Synopsis
By EDWARD H. SCHAFER

FLOATING
WORLD
EDITIONS

LCC 60-10361
ISBN 1-891640-15-1

Published by Floating World Editions
1-860-868-0890
FloatingWorldEditions.com

Distributed byAntique Collectors' Club
1-800-252-5231
AntiqueCollectorsClub.com

TU WAN'S

STONE CATALOGUE

OF CLOUDY FOREST

杜綰

雲林石譜

To Donna Deering Schafer

CONTENTS

ILLUSTRATIONS
(following page 36)

A GROUP OF THE "EIGHTEEN LEARNED GENTLEMEN" OF
THE T'ANG DYNASTY

The work of an anonymous Sung painter. From *The Collection of the Calligraphy and Painting in the Old Palace
(Ku kung shu hua chi)*. Peip'ing, 1930–1936.

AUSPICIOUS DRAGON STONE

Attributed to Emperor Hui Tsung of Sung, but possibly
a twentieth-century forgery. From *Famous Relics in the
Hall of the Great Wind (Ta feng t'ang ming chi)*, Kyoto,
1955–1956.

A GROUP OF THE "EIGHTEEN LEARNED GENTLEMEN" OF
THE T'ANG DYNASTY

By another unknown Sung artist. From *The Collection
of the Calligraphy and Painting in the Old Palace (Ku
kung shu hua chi)*, Peip'ing, 1930–1936.

The chapter vignettes of fantastic stones are reproduced
from the woodcuts in the early seventeenth-century book
Stone Catalogue of the Plain Garden (Su yüan shih p'u)
by Lin Yu-lin, republished in 1933. They purport to show
stones from the collection of the painter Mi Fu.

ONE

The Chinese Taste in Stones

In China, as elsewhere, stones were important to human welfare in the most remote times, especially as tools, but we cannot now tell to what extent the men of the Palaeolithic and Neolithic eras admired stones for their own sake, independently of their use as tools. In early historic times, however, a few hints emerge. The "Tribute of Yü," for instance, which reflects a rather dim image of commerce in the middle of the first millennium B.C., includes articles called "fantastic stones" (*kuai shih* 怪石) in its classic repertory of "tribute" due the Son of Heaven. But although Chinese literature between the Chou and Sung dynasties contains many incidental references to stones both as esthetic objects and as raw material for useful artifacts, no book entirely about stones, with either emphasis, appears before the twelfth century of our era. The "Stone Catalogue of Cloudy

Forest" (*Yün lin shih p'u*) is the first such book, and it is primarily concerned with stones which are excellent in themselves. That is to say, it is in the tradition of the attitude expressed, it seems, by the entry in the "Tribute of Yü."

But the term "fantastic stones" in the *Yü kung*, and also in the *Shan hai ching*, a book of similar antiquity, was taken in Han times to refer to ornamental semiprecious stones, not to garden rocks of curious shapes, as in later times. In his gloss on this phrase K'ung An-kuo, the classical scholiast of the first and second centuries B.C., wrote, "a fantastic, strange and attractive stone, resembling jade." We must ask, then, when did this expression begin to lose its specific reference to a gem stone (in the broadest sense) from Shantung and begin to refer to eroded limestones and other rocks suggestive of miniature landscapes? The answer is not readily found.

By T'ang times, certainly, the term was generally used in the second meaning. But usage during the first six centuries of our era is uncertain: when the *Chin shu*[1] tells of "the stocks of lacquer and silk in Yen and Yü; the stores of fantastic stones in Yen and Ch'i," we are unsure what stones these are. It is very likely that we have in this text only a classical metaphor for ornamental stones generally. In any case, it seems that the new usage developed slowly between the third and the sixth centuries, and became firmly established in gardener's language during the T'ang period, let us say from the seventh or eighth century.[2]

Meanwhile, through the two millennia intervening between the *Yü kung* and the *Yün lin shih p'u*, much was written about

---

[1] "Shih huo chih," 26, 1153b. In this book, all page references to the Dynastic Histories are to the *K'ai ming* edition. Three abbreviations are employed throughout: SPTK for *Szu pu ts'ung k'an*, TSCC for *Ts'ung shu chi ch'eng*, and YTCS for *Yü ti chi sheng*.

[2] The twelfth-century critic Ch'eng Ta-ch'ang argued that the Han scholiasts did not really know what kind of stone this was. Ch'eng himself was certain that it was nothing like the perforated esthetic objects called "fantastic stones" in his own day; he believed it to be some useful substance having the qualities of stone, but not stone at all. See *Yen fan lu*, 3, 12b-13a (*Hsüeh chin t'ao yüan* ed.).

stones and minerals in books of a more general character. One of the earliest of these was the *Fan tzu Chi jan*, a treatise on basic economics and natural history, composed in the fifth century B.C. by Fan Li. This work, which since the T'ang dynasty has survived only in fragments with interpolated Han place names, gave information on the minerals of China. Other ancient books reflect varying interests in stones: the *Kuan tzu*, possibly of the third century B.C., contains notes on mining along with many other economic and technical matters, while the *Shan hai ching* undoubtedly comprises Chou materials in its listings of pigment minerals, ornamental stones, and musical stones.

The best Chinese knowledge of rocks and minerals, however, is preserved in the long series of pharmacopoeias, beginning with the *Shen nung pen ts'ao ching*, the prototype of its kind. We now have only the edition made of this classic in the late fifth century by T'ao Hung-ching, but the form it had in Han times can be determined with reasonable certainty. It described the medicinal properties of a great variety of mineral substances, including cinnabar, quicksilver, azurite, mica, limonite, realgar, and sulphur. This kind of treatment of mineralogical and petrological data became the special province of the learned pharmacologists, quite independent of the esthetic interests of gentlemen like Tu Wan, the author of the *Yün lin shih p'u*. In the latter treatise, and in its congeners, such as the various poems in praise of attractive or remarkable stones, we find little trace of the magical and none of the medical preoccupations which characterize both the Chinese pharmacopoeias and the Western lapidaria.

The origin of the love of stones for their own sake, or more precisely for their microcosmic mimicry of mountain landscapes, must be looked for in the ancient interest in stones shaped naturally like living creatures: a tortoise, a horse, a man, or the Buddha, and in fossiliferous rocks containing "stone swallows" and other monsters. Such aberrations of the vital fluids of Nature are frequently mentioned in pre-T'ang literature. Reinforcing the fascination such objects always had for the Chinese was a mass of folklore about haunted stones in wild rugged places, curiously shaped rocks associated with dragons, devils, saints, and gods.[3] It was only necessary to transfer a strangely formed stone, or a stone with an attached legend, to an urban garden, to accomplish the innovation in taste. Add to this a sophisticated intuition of the structure of the world and the operations of "Heaven" subtly suggested by the contours of a picturesque rock, and we have the attitude of the T'ang or Sung connoisseur full-fledged.

This tinge of cosmology in the design of medieval gardens had antecedents in ancient magic as well. As stones might symbolize mountains, so gardens might represent the world in miniature. The great parks of the Han emperors seem to have figured a subcelestial (*t'ien hsia* 天下) realm on a reduced scale. Planted with the flora of the four quarters, stocked with the fauna of the several provinces, they confirmed and assured, by microcosmic imitation, the hold of the Son of Heaven on his universal domain. In the second century B. C., Ssu-ma Hsiang-ju idealized, in elaborate and florid images, the great park of the Han monarch Wu Ti. Writing of it as if he were describing the geography of China itself, he tells of the great rivers, which ". . . butt on vaulted rocks, and dash on dunes and bights." Indeed his rhapsody, *Shang lin fu*, abounds in allusions to rocks and stones: ". . . the water gems in boulder rubble," and ". . . the platy rocks and plaited cliffs." [4] Even minerals of decorative use or economic importance are placed within this paradise, as if they were samples displayed at a county fair.[5] Whether or not "His Highness' Forest" existed just as depicted by the great poet, it is certain that the idea of such a design was there.

The imaging of an entire mountain in a single rock was, it

---

[3] Examples of petrolatry are abundant. Many may be found in W. Eberhard, *Lokalkulturen im alten China*, Pt. I (*T'oung Pao*, Suppl. to Vol. 37, Leiden, 1942), and Pt. II (*Monumenta Serica*, Monograph Series, Peking, 1942).

[4] *Shih chi*, 117, 0255d, 0256a-b.

[5] Especially in the *Tzu hsü fu*.

seems, a conception which was not fully matured until T'ang times. But the creation of a miniature mountain in a garden goes back to the early part of the Six Dynasties period, probably even to the Han. The romantic *Hsi ching tsa chi*,[6] in describing the elaborate garden of a wealthy man, purportedly of the Han dynasty, tells how ". . . he fashioned stones to make a mountain, more than ten *chang* [one hundred feet] high." Whether or not they were built on such a gigantic scale as this, the rocky hills of Six Dynasties gardens were probably of this type; that is, they were essentially heaps of stones. The language of the *Sung shu* points to such a construction when it tells of the gardens of the gentry of the early fifth century, where ". . . they amass stones, draw in water, and plant groves."[7] During this age the concept of the garden mountain, already embodying the ancient Chinese worship of holy and cosmic mountains, was strengthened by Buddhist cosmology; the rockery could be a replica of Mount Sumeru, populated with images of the deities.[8]

In T'ang times, however, the advanced connoisseur replaced this rock-pile mountain with a single monumental stone. The latter was not a naturalistic representation of a mountain, but a symbolic and ideal image. As Sirén put it, ". . . their function

---

[6] *SPTK* ed., 3, 2b. The same source places an artificial mountain in the garden of Prince Liu Wu of Han. See Liang Ch'i-hsiung, "Che chiang lu," *Chung-kuo ying-tsao–hsüeh-she hui-k'an*, 4, 3-4 (June, 1934), 221-222. This article contains the biographies of Chinese landscape architects from Han to modern times.

[7] *Sung shu*, 93, 1644a. Fifth-century gardens, and later ones as well, were not necessarily natural. Hsiao Pao-chüan, for instance, the sybaritic prince who ruled Ch'i briefly at the end of the century, had a lavish garden with a mountain of stones painted in polychrome. (*Nan Ch'i shu*, 7, 1676a).

[8] Loraine W. Kuck, *The Art of Japanese Gardens* (New York, 1940), p. 10. Readers interested in the cosmological and mythological aspects of Chinese garden design are referred to R. Stein's learned and pleasant monograph, "Jardins en miniature d'Extrême-Orient," *BEFEO*, 42 (1943), 1-104. Although this essay treats chiefly of the history of miniature gardens and dwarfed trees in the Far East, a vogue which seems to date from the early T'ang in China, and spread to Japan and Annam, Stein has also much to say of stones.

was to serve as a substitute for the wonderful landscapes seen in dreams. . . ." [9]

Yet, though many books on natural history written during the Six Dynasties and T'ang epochs are concerned in part with stones, these are typically only small ornamental and precious stones, ores and reagents, pigments and drugs. They tell us very little about stones employed in building or carved into utensils, or about rocks admired for the beauty of their natural shape and color. This latter kind of interest, fully manifest in the "Stone Catalogue of Cloudy Forest," was, before the twelfth century, revealed only in poems and literary essays. Before the Sung dynasty, the ordinary form for monographic treatment of a special feature of nature or culture was the "rhapsody," the *fu* (賦). Many such highly embellished fantasies on the subject of stones survive. An instance is the "Rhapsody on Stones" (*Shih fu*) of Li Yung (A.D. 678–747). Presumably similar poetic essays existed even in Han times. The catalogue of literature in the *Han shu* refers to eighteen collections of "Miscellaneous Rhapsodies on Mountains, Tumuli, Water, Foam, Clouds, Vapors, Rain, and Droughts," then extant. In T'ang, at least, there were also prose essays in praise of individual rocks. Such was Po Chü-i's "Record of the Stone of Grand Lake," written in the ninth century in justification of the hobby of the author's friend Niu Seng-ju, the outstanding amateur of stones of the T'ang period.

Though stones, admired for their beauty or oddity, had already been used in some fashion in the gardens of the Six Dynasties period, and more carefully in the semiformal gardens of early T'ang aristocrats,[10] the ninth century was the age of the

---

[9] O. Sirén, *Gardens of China* (New York, 1949), p. 11.

[10] Murakami Yoshimi, "Tō-dai kizoku no teien," *Tōhōgaku*, 11 (1955), 76-77. In this and other essays, Murakami has shown the parallel but divergent development of the formal and "natural" styles in China. The "formal" garden was more architectural, and more ornamented with recognizable artifacts. An extreme example, if it actually existed, was the garden of silk flowers in Canton, reported by a Muslim sailor, perhaps in the tenth century. See *The Book of the Marvels of India* (London, 1928),

first great connoisseurs of stones. Among these the most notable
were Li Te-yü and Niu Seng-ju. Both of these eminent rivals had
famous gardens. That of Li Te-yü will be noticed again, when
we come to the description of one of his landscape stones in Tu
Wan's catalogue. Niu Seng-ju decorated the garden of the home
he built in Loyang in A.D. 837 with "fantastic stones" brought
from Huai-nan, and was accustomed to read poetry there in
company with Po Chü-i.[11]

In the eleventh and twelfth centuries the vogue for writing
factual studies of natural objects, precisely classified, was current. These compilations were commonly called "catalogues"
(譜). With or without this name, many well-known
works belong to this class—books such as the painter Mi Fu's
"History of Palettes." It is to this fashion that we owe the lapidarium of Tu Wan. Among the notable rock fanciers of early
Sung was Mi Fu himself, and his eleventh-century contemporary,
Su Shih.[12] This eminent poet wrote sixteen poems specifically
about decorative rocks,[13] and references to these verses are
abundant in Tu Wan's Stone Catalogue. Such was the value
that Su placed on fine specimens that he was unwilling to part
with his two "Ch'ou-ch'ih Stones" for anything of less worth
than a pair of horse paintings by the T'ang master Han Kan.[14]

---

p. 112. In the present essay I am only concerned with the "natural" taste
in garden design, however contrived that may have been.

[11] Chiu T'ang shu, 172, 3525d.

[12] Both men are frequently alluded to in colophons to Tu Wan's treatise, and in other later lapidaria. Thus Chu Chiu-ting (fl. 1659) wrote in
the preface to his own catalogue of stones: "Men of antiquity, such as Mi
Yüan-chang and Su Tung-p'o, often had a mania for stones."

[13] The section ch'üan shih 泉石 in chap. 8, pp. 15b–32a of Chi chu
fen lei Tung-p'o hsien-sheng shih (in SPTK) contains thirty-one stanzas,
almost equally divided between "springs" and "rocks."

[14] See the series of poems and their prefaces (ibid., 8, 23a–26a). There
was a considerable controversy among Su and his friends about a jocular
(?) proposal of Wang Chin-ch'ing to steal the stones. The eccentric wag
Chiang Ying-shu thought that the best solution was to "burn the paintings and smash the stones." The atmosphere of the narrative suggests that
this action would be comparable to burning the Mona Lisa and smashing
the Venus de Milo.

This not uncommon craze spread to the highest in the land. The last of the Northern Sung sovereigns, Hui Tsung, was a notorious petromaniac. His greatest single collecting effort was related to the construction of a magic mountain to the northeast of the imperial palace at K'ai-feng, at the urging of a geomancer. The completion of this monumental undertaking required several years, having been begun in A.D. 1117. To it were brought stones of wonderful shape from all parts of the realm, especially those of the Grand Lake and of Ling-pi.[15] These seem in part to have been used for the actual construction of the mountain, which, like the cosmic parks of the Han emperors, was populated with exotic birds and beasts, and in part as specimen stones, smaller analogues of the total construction, along the pathways leading through it. Doubtless the whole formed a diagram of the seen and unseen universes, embellished esthetically in accordance with the prevailing vogue for specimen stones. The monarch's unabating passion for such marvels in his parks and gardens provided a profitable business for the collector Chu Mien, who marshaled the resources of the empire, including even warships, to bring rare specimens to the august connoisseur, who amassed an enormous collection both of grotesque garden rocks and of fine lapidary work in semiprecious stones. Hui Tsung seems not to have been overscrupulous in requisitioning notable examples of stones from his subjects. The Catalogue tells repeatedly of privately owned specimens which were transferred to the palace during the first two decades of the twelfth century. Chu Mien was showered with honors and dignities for such services. The Roman Caligula, when he dignified his horse Incitatus with the title of Consul, ennobled a living creature; Hui Tsung extended a similar honor to the mineral kingdom, and formally enfeoffed a prodigious stone as "Marklord of P'an-ku." [16] In such an era it was inevitable that

---

[15] See *Sung shih*, 85, 4700c, and especially Chang Hao (fl. 1216), *Ken yüeh chi* (in *Ku chin shuo hai*). The Grand Lake and Ling-pi stones are discussed in Tu Wan's catalogue; see below, Nos. 4 and 1.

[16] *Sung shih*, 470, 5674a, and Fang Shuo, *Po che pien* (*Pai hai* ed.), b, 6a. P'an-ku was a primordial cosmogonic deity, fashioner of the earth and its rocky bones.

a book like the *Yün lin shih p'u* would be produced. What is surprising is that a book of such unique character should have been so much neglected by Sinologists. Osvald Sirén ignores it in his treatment of Chinese garden rocks;[17] Berthold Laufer mistakenly refers to it as "a treatise on economic mineralogy." [18]

Doubtless it is not the proper part of a scholar to make value judgments about the taste of another age and another tradition. Yet a few remarks of this character may not be out of place if they serve, corrected for our own perspective, to point up the special quality or "atmosphere" of a phase of culture. Two classes of stone were singled out for enjoyment and praise by the most cultivated persons of late medieval China. The first of these indicates a "baroque," the second a "primitive" taste. Under the rubric "baroque" I count the pseudonatural garden stone. There is no question about the bizarreness of the most celebrated specimens of this group. Tu Wan, and other writers as well, repeatedly describe choice examples in such terms as *"odd"* (*i* 異), *"singular"* (*ch'i* 奇) and *"fantastic"* (*kuai* 怪). That these words were well chosen is borne out by Ming prints and paintings of aristocratic gardens, some containing very old stones. The second group, which I have styled "primitive," includes objects on a much smaller scale which, though interesting and even attractive to many of our own generation and tradition, would not be regarded now as worthy of serious attention as art objects, but only as curious or quaint. I refer, of course, to stones which are endowed with the shapes or stained with the silhouettes of alien things, whether natural or artificial. Tu Wan describes many of these: chalcedony pebbles shaped like a tortoise or a deity; moss agate and other minerals naturally painted with the contours of forests or of clouds; stalactites in the image of drum or dragon. It is rather surprising to read of the great sums paid for such esthetic trifles, and of the enormous esteem in which they were held by educated gentlemen and arbiters of taste. Yet it cannot be doubted that these prefer-

---

[17] *Gardens of China.*

[18] In Frank P. Wiborg, *Printing Ink* (New York and London, 1926), p. 15.

ences were often the source of genuine poetic and even meta-physical inspiration—"sermons in stones," as the Duke said in *As You Like It*. Liu Tsung-yüan's (eighth and ninth centuries) beautiful essay "Record of the Mountain of the Little Walled City of Stone" is a case in point. Such genuine appreciation of landscape fits the criterion of Santayana, given in his *Sense of Beauty:* "A landscape to be seen has to be composed, and to be loved has to be moralized," while at the same time matching, sometimes, the same philosopher's conception of the grotesque: ". . . if . . . we have an inkling of the unity and character in the midst of the strangeness of the form, then we have the grotesque." Therefore, though at worst these simulacra were simply curious museum pieces, at best they were fairy worlds complete. Even at best, however, the baroque character of this taste is evident. In an age of great painters and appreciation of great painting, Su Tung-p'o (Su Shih) could say of the patterns on his treasured agates: "Even though an artist might aim to delineate and depict them, he would be unable to achieve this." [19] Poetry about such stones, and paintings of them, common in these times, find perfect analogues in written and plastic encomiums of antique sculpture in the modern Western world.[20]

---

[19] Said of the Stones of Huang-*chou* (Article 91, below). Compare Isaac D'Israeli on a stone showing the image of an old man's head: "beautiful as if the hand of Raphael had designed it." (*Curiosities of Literature,* [9th ed.; London, 1834], I, 361.) A good account of the baroque element in Chinese taste may be found in Hans H. Frankel, "Poetry and Painting: Chinese and Western Views of Their Convertibility," *Comparative Literature,* 9 (1957), 289–307. The reader is also referred to Jurgis Baltrušaitis, *Aberrations; quatre essais sur la légende des formes* (Paris, 1957), especially pp. 47–72: "Pierres imagées," a study of jaspers, marbles, and agates with the shadows of the visible world in them, and pp. 97–125: "Jardins et pays d'illusion," a study of Anglo-Chinese gardens and their "scènes enchantées."

[20] We have noted that picturesque stones figure importantly in the poetry of this era. It is not surprising that they were also subjects for the painter. The Sung landscapist Kuo Hsi, for instance, did two pictures of "*Artistic* stones with paired pines," and two of "*Singular* stones with wintry forest." The latter subject also attracted the attention of Li Ch'eng, who

We speak of *le goût anglo-chinois* of the eighteenth century as exemplifying the "exotic" and the "grotesque" tastes. We are prone to believe that the "grotesque" quality was imposed on the original Chinese, that the misshapen character of fashionable garden construction in that epoch reveals the unhappy degeneration of a pure and admirable style, native to the Far East. Though unavoidably altered in transition, the original Chinese taste was already grotesque. So far as rockeries are concerned, at any rate, the European examples are no more bizarre than the Chinese. Indeed, the rugged masses of rock on which "Chinese" pavilions were placed in the age of Louis XV and Louis XVI seem quite unostentatious when compared with the eccentric garden stones of the Ming dynasty. In a few instances we detect an almost authentically Chinese touch, as in the eighteenth-century rockery at Painshill Park in Surrey, England, riddled with holes in the best Sung tradition.[21] The one feature of Chinese stone appreciation which caught on best in Europe, however, was the mysterious grotto. The rocky entrance to the Désert de Monville, the present Désert de Retz near Paris, though inhabited by fauns instead of Taoist sylphs, and many other artificial caverns of the eighteenth century, would have found sympathetic interest in a Chinese of the twelfth century, though the latter would have preferred a natural limestone cave. In some ways, the Chinese preference for massive distorted stones and rock piles found more ready acceptance in Europe than in Japan, where the miniature garden or more self-effacing

---

created in addition a set of "*Gigantic* stones with wintry forest." (Italics mine.) See *Hsüan ho shih p'u* (in *TSCC* ed.), 11, 287–291, and 304.

[21] O. Sirén, *China and the Gardens of Europe of the Eighteenth Century* (New York, 1950), plate 38. The love of grottoes in Europe had also classical origins, and the splendid grottoes of seventeenth-century Italy and England, with their "water conceits," can ultimately be traced to the ancient grottoes of Diana. The elaborate eighteenth-century revival introduced a strong Chinese tone. See the survey in Geoffrey Grigson and Charles Harvard Gibbs-Smith, *Things; a Volume of Objects Devised by Man's Genius which are the Measure of His Civilization* (New York [n.d.]), pp. 186–188.

collection of stones became traditional.[22] Even the vogue for small specimens of fantastic stones displayed on a wooden taboret or in a metal bowl, current in Sung times, left a trace in European culture: among the so-called "Jesuit watercolors" in the Bibliothéque Nationale is an album of colored pictures of "Pierres Employées pour Ornemens dans les Jardins chinois," which are "colorful stones of bizarre shapes in porcelain jars." This fashion seems not to have become widespread, however.[23]

The so-called "English" taste in rock arrangements, then, though assigned to the "grotesque" style by us, inherited its grotesqueness lawfully from the ancestral Chinese taste. Even more: the "Chinese" garden which appealed so deeply to the romantic sensibility of the eighteenth century was, even in its antecedents, not natural at all, as I shall attempt to show presently. Even Sir William Chambers, who had seen Chinese gardens first hand, and whose *Dissertation on Oriental Gardening* was so influential in shaping the trend of landscape gardening in his day, recognized that the supposedly informal gardens of China were in fact highly contrived.[24]

In short, the Chinese baroque, if I may use such a novel term, was not natural to begin with, and was not unduly exaggerated by its European imitators.

---

[22] See Samuel Newsom, *A Thousand Years of Japanese Gardens* (Tokyo, 1957), p. 66.

[23] Eleanor von Erdberg, *Chinese Influence on European Garden Structures* (Cambridge, Mass., 1936), pp. 25–26.

[24] William Chambers, *A Dissertation on Oriental Gardening* (London, 1772). Chambers gives an excellent description of the kind of fantastic stone so much admired in China: "They also introduce in their lakes large artificial rocks, built of a particular fine coloured stone, found on the sea-coasts of China, and designed with much taste. These are pierced with many openings through which you discover distant prospects; and have in them caverns for the reception of crocodiles, enormous water-serpents, and other monsters; cages for rare aquatic birds; and grottos, with many shining apartments, adorned with marine productions, and gems of various sorts."

TWO

Tu Wan, Author of the Stone Catalogue

Other than what we can glean from his own pages and what is told of him in the preface to his catalogue, written by his contemporary, K'ung Ch'uan, we know nothing of Tu Wan. Like the editors who composed colophons to the catalogue in later times, K'ung Ch'uan was anxious to justify a special study of stones as objects of esthetic contemplation. He pointed out that no similar book was in existence, though the type was well known, examples being Ou-yang Hsiu's monograph on tree-peonies and Ts'ai Hsiang's catalogue of lichee varieties, both written in the eleventh century. Stones, he says, are well worth study, since they purify the imagination: did not the Master himself say, "The humane person finds happiness in the mountains," and is not the love of rocks an instance of this, and a suitable devotion for a Confucian gentleman? [25]

From this we can understand why this book has been preserved since the twelfth century. K'ung Ch'uan and others like him cared little for precious stones as frivolous articles of adornment, or for rocks as working materials for hard-handed artisans, or for mineral drugs prescribed by lowly physicians, or for reagents necessary to the vain pursuits of alchemists. For the gentleman, a stone, as a microcosmic mountain, suggests nobility, patience, stability, seclusion, and the virtuous contemplation of nature. K'ung Ch'uan tells us what should be done with stones: "If large, they may be set out in garden and hospice; if small, they may be placed on table or stand." Properly one does not do things *with* stones; it is sufficient that they inspire lofty moods. All of this is the more understandable in view of the fact that K'ung Ch'uan was a direct descendant of Confucius.[26]

Although the elevated reputation of its subject may have helped the book to survive until the twentieth century, while many Taoist writings on natural history have perished, the book does not in fact live up to the reputation. Tu Wan is embarrassingly matter of fact in his treatment of rocks. He tells where they are found, and how they are excavated; he describes their shape, color, and properties; he comments on the pleasant sounds they emit when struck; and, although he does not descend to medicine, magic, or fripperies, he remarks casually enough where the stones he describes are employed: for such lowly purposes as repairing walls, making household utensils, and even for ladies' cosmetics. Indeed almost two-thirds of the catalogue concerns stones used in handicrafts, though the landscape stones occupy the place of honor in the first chapter. It is also characteristic that our author shows no "scientific" interest in stones. His laconic descriptions of their physical properties are only guides

---

[25] The classical precedent for this attitude is found in the metaphorical eulogy of jade in the *K'ung tzu chia yü*, section 36 "Inquiry about Jade," (chap. 8 of *Tzu shu po chia* ed.)

[26] K'ung Ch'uan is best known for his continuation of Po Chü-i's encyclopedia *Lu t'ieh*.

to the collector or connoisseur. His fascinating explanation of the fossil fish of Ch'ang-sha is, after all, only a passing speculation, not a carefully stated theory. The genteel employment of a stone is of much more importance to him than its genesis, even when he remarks its use among the plebs. Chang Hai-p'eng, who wrote a colophon to the Stone Catalogue at the beginning of the nineteenth century, was more realistic about the contents of the book than K'ung Ch'uan. He admits, as Tu Wan himself does, that the role of stones in the life of a cultivated person is more than a passive one: they are important as the raw material of ink palettes (often called "inkslabs" or "inkstones" by writers on China), screens, private seals, and are employed in lithography. All these things enter into the life of a *literatus*, and it was this highly specialized but not purely contemplative life that Tu Wan had chiefly in mind.

K'ung Ch'uan tells us that Tu Wan had the byname Chi-yang, and that he was also styled Yün lin chü shih, "Gentleman Resident in Cloudy Forest," an epithet also borne in the fourteenth century by the landscape painter Ni Tsan. He also observes that Tu Wan must have been a collector of stones. This is a reasonable inference. It is difficult to understand otherwise how he could have described so many in such detail. Indeed, the catalogue tells of his travels in search of specimens, and how he acquired them. Stone collecting was apparently a hobby of the Tu family, since Tu Wan refers to examples in the possession both of his late father and of his younger brother.

Other than this, nothing of Tu Wan's life and livelihood has been reported. His lineage, however, is taken note of: he was a descendant of the great T'ang poet Tu Fu,[27] and a grandson of the illustrious eleventh-century statesman, Tu Yen.[28] The title

---

[27] All editions have *I-t'ang hsien-sheng* 抑堂先生 , an otherwise unreported name of the poet. I am grateful to Mrs. Chung-ho Frankel for the suggestion that *i* 抑 is a corruption of *ts'ao* 艸 , a variant of 草 .

[28] K'ung Ch'uan stirred up a teapot tempest by remarking in his preface that Tu Wan's celebrated ancestor has a line in his set of "Sundry Poems on Ch'in-*chou*" referring to "fish and dragons." He sees a connection

page of most editions of his book give Shan-yin in Shao-hsing as his native place. It is certain that his grandfather came from there, but Tu Wan's own name does not even appear in the Chekiang gazetteer.

So much we can depend on. But it may be that Tu Wan was a public as well as a private collector. It is clear from the contents of his catalogue that he was familiar with the imperial stone collection. Perhaps there was good reason for this. Such passages as the following about a particularly fine specimen occur in his book: "During 'Exalted Peace' [A.D. 1102–1106] it was desired to bring it by cart and install it in the Interior Repository, but since there were many words and phrases carved on the back of the stone by earlier persons, some of which were tabooed at this time, this was, in consequence, suspended." This suggests the possibility that Tu Wan himself was an imperial agent, who gained his intimate knowledge of the famous stones of the realm by canvassing the collections of private citizens, maybe even hand in glove with the rapacious Chu Mien. Perhaps, even, the *Yün lin shih p'u* is actually a descriptive list of the stones in the imperial collection, an hypothesis that gains some support from the frequency with which the author writes that the stone he is discussing has been taken into the "Interior Repository" (*nei fu* 內府). The theory would also explain how Tu Wan can describe, in the minutest detail, the attributes of the rarest stones in the land, worthy of and sought by royalty.

All this is mere speculation, but there is a modicum of support for it. The *Che chiang t'ung chih*[29] quotes a book called *Hsüan ho shih p'u* in several places.[30] Examination of the quoted passages shows that they are identical with the received text of

---

between this and Tu Wan's description of "Fish and Dragon Stone," a fossiliferous rock from the vicinity of Ch'ang-sha, and a similar rock from the region of Lung-hsi, that is, of Ch'in-*chou*. The editors of the *Szu k'u ch'üan shu tsung mu* take considerable pains to point out that Kansu is not Hunan, as if they had not read the whole of Tu Wan's article and so had missed his reference to the stone fish of Lung-hsi.

[29] In 1934 photolith of 1899 edition, based on 1736 edition.

[30] Chaps. 101–107, *wu-ch'an.* 物產

the *Yün lin shih p'u*.[31] In short, for the editors of the gazetteer, *Hsüan ho shih p'u* and *Yün lin shih p'u* are alternate titles for the same book. It seems as if these worthies had access to an edition of Tu Wan's catalogue which differed from all extant editions in being called "The Stone Catalogue of Promulgated Accord." This title makes a set with the well-known anonymous compendia *Hsüan ho shu p'u* and *Hsüan ho hua p'u*, catalogues of the specimens of calligraphy and painting which Hui Tsung kept in his gallery at the Basilica of Promulgated Accord.[32] It seems unlikely, though not impossible, that the *t'ung chih* editors simply made an idle mistake in citation, and then repeated it many times.

There was, in fact, another book named *Hsüan ho shih p'u*. A fragment of this survives in the *Shuo fu* collections. The 1647 edition of the *Shuo fu* attributes it to a certain Ch'ang Mao, and the *Ming ch'ao pen* version attributes it to a priest named Tsu-k'ao. But this mutilated text, as given in both sources, is virtually identical with passages in the *Hua-yang Kung chi shih*, the work of the priest Tsu-hsiu. The latter book is not a true catalogue, but a description of Hui Tsung's rockeries written, after the emperor's abdication, as a pretext for pious moralizing. "Tsu-k'ao" must be none other than Tsu-hsiu, and the fragmentary "Stone Catalogue of Promulgated Accord" must be identical with the "Record of Matters at the Hua-yang Palace." Though it contains interesting information, such as the names bestowed by the monarch on his favorite stones and engraved on their surfaces in letters of gold, or, for less worthy specimens, in blue characters, it is evidently not a proper analogue of the catalogues of painting and calligraphy.[33]

It does not necessarily follow that Tu Wan's book is an official catalogue: it is neither polite nor courtly. But it does seem

---

[31] Some quotations are cited as from *Yün lin shih p'u*. The choice of title seems quite arbitrary.

[32] See F. Hirth, "Bausteine zu einer Geschichte der Chinesischen Literatur," *T'oung Pao*, 7 (1896), 482.

[33] The *Hua-yang Kung chi shih* may be found in *ts'e* 116 of *Hsüeh hai lei pien*.

to be an unofficial, descriptive, and systematic manual, drawing heavily on the imperial collections for its material, and written for the benefit of connoisseurs by Tu Wan.

Specifically against this possibility is the silence of all persons who have studied Tu Wan's book, including K'ung Ch'uan, author of the preface of 1133, and the editors of the *Szu k'u ch'üan shu tsung mu.*

Note.—Since this essay was put in the hands of the publisher, I have learned of the existence of an unpublished German translation of the *Yün lin shih p'u,* the doctoral dissertation of Dr. Helmut Bendig, accepted in 1950. The full reference is Helmut Bendig, *Das Yün-lin-shih-p'u: Ein Beitrag zur Kulturgeschichte der Sung-Zeit* (Inaugural-Dissertation, Ph.D., *Rheinische* Friedrich Wilhelms-Universität zu Bonn [n.d.]). I have been able to consult this typescript through the courtesy of Professor Herbert Franke. Pages 59–60 (note 309) show, for example, that Tu Wan relied heavily on *Yang Wen-kung t'an yüan (ca.* 1000) for his description of *Bodhisattva Stone* (my No. 89), a fact that I had not observed. Such textual criticism forms a valuable part of Dr. Bendig's dissertation.

THREE

History and Character of the Text

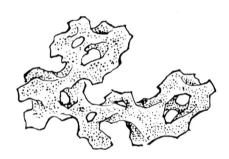

The latest possible year for the composition of the Stone Catalogue of Cloudy Forest is A.D. 1133, the date of K'ung Ch'uan's
preface. Internal evidence, including place names, shows that it
must have been completed a few years earlier.

(1) All editions give the place of origin of the first stone in
the catalogue as *Ling-pi,* written 靈壁 . This form was not
adopted until A.D. 1117, replacing *Ling-pi, written* 零壁 . The
book is therefore later.

(2) The name Hsi-ch'ing-*fu* appears twice, for old Yen-*chou;*
it was adopted in 1118. The book is later.

(3) The author writes "Tuan-*chou,* which is now Chao-
ch'ing—*fu,*" a name adopted in 1118. The book is later.

(4) Events of the reign "Promulgated Accord" are referred
to more than once, in language indicating that the author was

not writing during that reign. The book was finished after the period 1119–1125.

(5) Hsü-i-*hsien* and Chao-hsin-*hsien* are given as subdivisions of Szu-*chou*. They were removed from this jurisdiction in 1130. The book was completed before that year.

(6) The text has "Lin-an-*hsien* in Hang-*chou*," which was redesignated Lin-an-*fu* in 1129. The book was written before this date.

(7) "Stones of the Lo River" are found near the "Western Capital," that is, Lo-yang. This city was abandoned as the Sung imperial residence when it was taken by the Jurchen in 1126. The book was completed this year or earlier.

From this it seems that the most likely period for the completion of the catalogue was A.D. 1126–1130. The most probable year is 1126, though a year as late at 1130 is possible if the author was careless in his use of the official toponymy.[34]

Modern versions of the text fall into four lines of descent, which I have labeled A, B, C, and D.

(A)   This version is found in the *Shuo fu* of 1647, whence it was copied almost verbatim into the *Ku chin t'u shu chi ch'eng* of 1728. This is an inferior text, full of errors. It incorporates three articles from an entirely separate book, and omits four articles which appear in all other editions. The three interpolations belong in the *Yü yang Kung shih p'u*, a short work by an anonymous Sung author, which followed the *Yün lin shih p'u* in

---

[34] There is a contradictory piece of evidence. Tu Wan uses the name Ching-nan-*fu* for a place usually known under Sung as Chiang-ling-*fu*. According to *Sung shih* (88, 4709b), the title Ching-nan-*fu* was adopted in A.D. 1130 and abolished in 1135, to be restored again in 1174. This does not agree with my other evidence, in that it indicates a date of composition for the Stone Catalogue between 1130 and 1133. But *YTCS*, 64, 4a, says nothing of the use of the title Ching-nan-*fu* before 1174, whereas *Hu-pei t'ung chih* (1929 ed., 1, 294), says that the name Ching-nan-*fu* was first adopted in 1174, but on a later page refers to the adoption in 1130! *YTCS* has other quotations indicating confusion about this usage. All we learn from this is that a single piece of internal evidence based on official political geography is not in itself sufficient to establish a date.

the original *Shuo fu*. A fragment of this catalogue remains under the correct title in the 1647 *Shuo fu*, but the three wandering articles (an extra "Stone of Ling-pi"; "Stone of Li Te-yü"; "The Palette Mountain"), have unaccountably been detached from the rest and incorporated into Tu Wan's book.[35]

(B)   This version is found in the *Ch'ün fang ch'ing wan* collection (first edition, 1654). It seems to be ancestral to the *Hsüeh chin t'ao yüan* edition of 1802–1804, though there are a few small differences. The latter has been reprinted in the *Mei shu ts'ung shu* of 1928. This seems to be very reliable.

(C)   This version was printed in the *Chih pu tsu chai ts'ung shu* in 1814 by Pao T'ing-po in order to preserve (as he tells us in his colophon) a manuscript book he saw in the possession of a certain Ma Wen at the latter's "Apartment of the Cloudy Stone Mountain." T'ing-po found errors in this text which he corrected from the version of the catalogue reproduced in the *Ku chin t'u shu chi ch'eng*. As a gesture of respect to Ma Wen, himself a stone fancier, he printed that gentleman's essay *Chou yün shih chi*, written in 1811, along with a picture, as an addendum to Tu Wan's classic. This version was reprinted with punctuation in the *Ts'ung shu chi ch'eng* series in 1936. Here the arrangement of articles seems to differ from the author's original plan: stones from the same region are placed together, whatever their qualities and use. The B series, on the other hand, apparently preserves the plan of the original, with garden stones together, inkstones together, and so on.

(D)   The confused A series descends somehow from an excellent version, a form of which was reprinted in the *Ming ch'ao pen* edition of the *Shuo fu* in 1927. This was a lead-type text based on partial copies of Ming originals kept in the Han fen lou repository. No doubt it reproduces rather faithfully the version of the original and lamented *Shuo fu* of the fourteenth century. In most respects it is like the B series.

---

[35] *Yün lin shih p'u* was included in the Ming collectanea *T'ang Sung ts'ung shu*, but the edition of the latter accessible to me has been printed from the same badly worn blocks as the *Shuo fu* of 1647. I cannot surmise its form in the two Ming editions.

In writing the present study, I used the *Hsüeh chin t'ao yüan* edition (B series), but have freely made emendations based on other editions, especially the *Ming ch'ao pen*. In general, I have not explained the reasons for such adoptions, in order to avoid excessive pedantry. My hypothetic filiation of editions is shown in the accompanying chart.

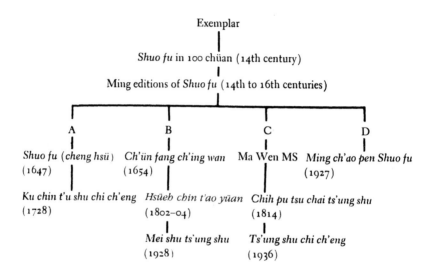

The special character of the descriptions of stones in the *Yün lin shih p'u* is best brought out by a comparison of one of these with the description of the same stone in a book of materia medica. Few comparable examples can be found, since most items in the lapidarium are *rocks*, whereas most in the pharmacopoeia are *minerals*. However, a few specific minerals do appear in the Stone Catalogue: among these are chalcedony, lapis-lazuli, limonite, turquoise, and malachite. It is convenient, then, to contrast the articles on malachite from the *Yün lin shih p'u* and from the *Ch'ung hsiu Cheng ho ching shih cheng lei pen ts'ao*, an approximately contemporary book.[36]

STONE GREEN (*Yün lin shih p'u*)

"The Stone Green of Ch'ien-shan-*hsien* ['Lead Mountain'] in Hsin-*chou* is produced within a deep pit. One species is fused and knotted to make the contours of mountain cliffs, but it is not very hard. One species is rather hard, with filaments brushed, as it were, extremely deep within the green color; this is gouged or milled to make utensils; when looked at facing the light, there is a considerable shining of splendent and flashing color. There is one more species which is pale green and sometimes finely fragmented; if boiled in water and pulverized, it is suitable for make-up ornamentation."

GREEN VERDITER OF HSIN-CHOU (*Cheng ho pen ts'ao*)

"Green verditer: taste, acid; cooling; nonpoisonous. Regime: augments the breath; cures catarrhs of the nose; inhibits diarrhoetic mixtures. Produced within pits on the shady sides of mountains. Color: bice-white.

T'ao the Dweller in Secret states:[37] "This is used for painting

---

[36] Actually the pharmacopoeia here translated is a thirteenth-century Japanese edition of a Chinese text of 1249, itself a revision of an original of 1116. I use the *SPTK* reprint, 3, 37a-b.

[37] T'ao Hung-ching, A.D. 452–536; his book of materia medica was written before 500.

green. It also comes from 'hollow verditer' [38] in which it is zoned and enclosed. Nowadays painting craftsmen call this 'prasine verditer,' [39] but hollow verditer they call 'green verditer,' though it is just the contrary!"

Annotations on the T'ang Basic Herbs[40] states: "Green verditer is 'laminate verditer.' [41] The painting craftsmen call it 'stone green,' while their 'prasine verditer' is 'white verditer.' It does not come into use in painting." [42]

The *Illustrated Canonical*[43] says: "Green verditer: nowadays we call it 'stone green.' Formerly they did not take note of the *chou* from whose soil it came, but stated only that it was produced 'within pits on the shady sides of mountains.' Under the article on hollow verditer in the *Basic Canon*[44] it is stated that it was produced in the mountains and valleys of I-*chou*, and in copper-bearing localities in the mountains of Yüeh-sui. This substance will have been produced on the shady sides of mountains. Nowadays it comes from Shao-*chou* and Hsin-*chou*. Its color is bice-white, and it is this which is used by painting craftsmen to paint green. When there are extremely large lumps, flowered and patterned attractively within bice-white, the people of Hsin-*chou* employ it to grind into rings for waist girdles and women's garments. When put into medicines, one should use pellets or lumps; the ones which are like 'nipple aromatic,'[45] unenclosed by stone, are the best. Medical practitioners today use it mostly as an expectorant for 'wind'-phlegms.[46] Their method is to make

---

[38] *k'ung ch'ing* 空青 , a form of azurite.

[39] *pi ch'ing* 碧青 . That is, painters call malachite "prasine verditer" rather than "green verditer."

[40] A popular name for the *Hsin hsiu pen ts'ao* of A.D. 659.

[41] *pien ch'ing* 扁青 .

[42] The coarse variety of malachite called "stone green" (as in the *Yün lin shih p'u*) is not used as a pigment. The fine-ground pale-green variety called "prasine verditer" by the painters, is also known as "white verditer." In earlier times (as by the poet Chiang Yen) "prasine marrow" was also a name for artist's malachite.

[43] The *Illustrated Canonical Basic Herbs* of A.D. 1601.

[44] Abbreviation for *The Canon of Basic Herbs of Shen Nung*, an edition of the Han classic done by T'ao Hung-ching in the fifth century.

[45] Nipple-like pellets of frankincense.

[46] Various diseases, especially those accompanied by chills and fevers, were called "winds."

a selection of the prime best, with superior color; it is first pounded and put through a sieve, then, by the repeated use of water flotation, the very finest is removed; it is then treated by further grinding. When there is a 'wind'-phlegm; with dizziness and anxiety, take two or three iron spoonfuls together with some three or four peas of fresh 'dragon brain' [camphor], and grind them until uniform; mix this in wine with the liquor of fresh peppermint; warm until blended, then swallow. Have [the patient] lie prone, and shortly the spittle will flow out from the corners of the mouth; then he will be cured, without vomiting or spitting up. Its effect is more rapid than other drugs. When men use it nowadays it is efficacious each and every time, and we have therefore appended this method here. An article below states further that 'laminate verditer' is produced in the mountains and valleys of Chu-yai [Hainan], and at Wu-tu [S.E. Kansu] and Chu-t'i [S. Szechwan]. Su Kung [seventh century; editor of T'ang pen ts'ao] states that this is in fact also green verditer. The kind which comes from Hainan is lump-shaped, as large as a fist. Its color is more blue, and sometimes even has hollows in the belly. We have not observed this color nowadays. It occurs also at Wu-ch'ang [in Hupeh], Chienᵃ-chou, and Tzuᵃ-chou [both in Szechwan]. These also have the same uses today."

The Amplified Interpretations[47] says: "Green verditer is in fact stone verditer. When this stone is black-bice in color it is best, and the larger ones are carved in the shapes of objects; at times it is used to make utensils. Also it has proved effective when tried, along with naushadir[48] [sal ammoniac], for expectorating 'wind'-phlegms, but then it is injurious to the heart."

The differences among these accounts are clear. Tu Wan is interested in malachite only as an ornamental stone. The herbal, on the other hand, although it alludes to sculpture in malachite, is primarily concerned with its medicinal properties, but also has much to say about its use, powdered, as a pigment. The pharmacopoeia also discusses the various names given to different kinds

---

[47] Short for Basic Herbs with Amplified Interpretations, the work of K'ou Tsung-shih, published A.D. 1116.

[48] See Laufer, Sino-Iranica, p. 504.

of malachite at different periods, and their alleged synonymity;
it is therefore of greater interest to the philologist. Finally, the
text of the herbal is almost entirely composed of quotations from
antecedent herbals, whereas the Stone Catalogue gives the
appearance of original writing.[49]

I am unable to find any evidence of connection between the
Stone Catalogue and the lapidaria of Islam. I am not competent
to handle the original texts of Kazwīnī, Bīrūnī, and Muhammad
ibn Mansūr, and must rely on published Western scholarship in
this field. The emphasis on magical and medicinal matters in the
lapidaries of the Muslims suggests somewhat the contents of the
Chinese pharmacopoeias, but they bear no resemblance to Tu
Wan's catalogue, either in plan or in detail.[50]

---

[49] At least I have seen no sources upon which Tu Wan might have
drawn. Ming and Ch'ing "stone catalogues," however, frequently imitate
the phraseology of Tu Wan, whose book had by then come to be regarded
as a classic. The interested reader may consult the descriptions of "Stone
of the Grand Lake" and others in the seventeenth-century *Yüan yeh*;
some of these have been translated by Sirén in his *Gardens*, pp. 24–28.
They show extensive "plagiarism" (no doubt of a reverent kind) from the
Stone Catalogue of Cloudy Forest. It is curious that Sirén, though he
considers the use of fantastic stones the most original and characteristic
feature of Chinese gardening, treats them very unhistorically. He observes
(p. 21) that the T'ai-hu stones were much admired in Sung, but not that
they were already collected in T'ang; he nowhere mentions Niu Seng-ju
as an early connoisseur; he has nothing to say about the *Yün lin shih p'u*.

[50] The trade in stones between East and West is a subject worthy of
study. Foreign stones, especially gem stones, were well known in China
(see my "Iranian Merchants in T'ang Dynasty Tales," in *Semitic and
Oriental Studies, Presented to William Popper, University of California
Publications in Semitic Philology*, Vol. XI, Berkeley and Los Angeles,
1951). Contrariwise, China was the supposed source of some stones admired by the Arabs. Thus the Arabic version of the lapidarium attributed
to Aristotle, representing a Syrian context of the ninth century, speaks of
the onyx of China as inferior to that of the Maghrib. See Julius Ruska,
Das Steinbuch des Aristoteles (Heidelberg, 1912). It may even be that
Chinese onyx reached as far as England: a twelfth-century Anglo-Norman
lapidary says of it, "D'Arabe e d'Inde sunt ces pieres" (P. Studer and
J. Evans, *Anglo-Norman Lapidaries* [Paris, 1924], p. 39.) Much needs to
be done in the way of collecting and interpreting such examples.

It cannot be denied that this international trade led to an exchange

It would be possible to classify the stones of the *Yün lin shih p'u* in various ways, none of them entirely satisfactory. A classification according to the species of rock is clearly impossible, owing to the absence of accurate petrological data. A classification by locality of origin, or by some physical characteristic, such as hardness or color, would be of little interest or value. The obvious arrangement is the best one: classification by manner of employment. All these rocks and minerals fall into two large classes: (1) those whose use is primarily esthetic, and (2) those whose use is primarily practical. These two categories are not mutually exclusive; some stones which are of suitable shape for a garden arrangement are, at the same time, susceptible to carving into useful objects. A more sophisticated analysis than the one I propose would take into account the fact that "esthetic" purposes are inextricably intermingled with "moral" notions, and that objects of "utilitarian" value, such as vases and palettes, are also art objects. Ignoring these interesting matters, we can further subdivide our stones as follows:

I. Esthetic

1. Realistic (resembling actual mountains, divinities, animals, etc.; dendriform markings on agate, etc.; also fossils).

2. Fantastic (bizarre shapes: cavernous, perforated, suggesting no real mountain, but appealing to the imagination as Taoist fairy grottoes, etc.).

3. Crystalline (composed of a single mineral, showing natural crystal forms).

4. Sensuous (as polished agate pebbles, lustrous to the eye, sleek to the touch).

5. Antiquarian (bearing old inscriptions, or associated with famous men or epochs).

6. Curiosities (having a legend attached).

---

or names of stones and of legends about stones. Indeed, F. de Mely, in his *Les Lapidaires de l'antiquité et du moyen âge*, Tome I: *Les Lapidaires chinois* (Paris, 1896), pp. lx-lxvi, which is chiefly based on Chinese sources of the fourteenth century and later, attempts to show examples of such interconnections. His effort is only moderately successful, but leads in the right direction.

II. Utilitarian

1. Cut into vessels and other utensils.
2. Sculpture: figurines, paperweights, etc.
3. Slabs for palettes, screens, chimes, etc.
4. Whetstones and touchstones, whose usefulness depends on surface texture.
5. Masonry.
6. Pigment, for painting and cosmetics.
7. Ancient artifacts, such as stone arrowheads.

Though not so systematic as the tabulations, the arrangement of Tu Wan's book is not haphazard. It shows rough groupings according to type: The "Upper Scroll" begins with my varieties I.1 and I.2, clearly regarded as superior, and then goes on to I.5. The "Middle" and "Lower Scrolls" describe types I.3, I.4, and the various types under II.

FOUR

Technology and Petrology

Some knowledge of the technology and the amateur science of the twelfth century may be gleaned from the pages of the Stone Catalogue. The few paragraphs which follow will give only a notion of this sort of information; full details must be sought in the book itself. It must be said, however, that Tu Wan seems to use the names of tools (for instance) rather loosely, and that the appearance of "gouge," "chisel," or "ax" may be due more to the needs of style than to the needs of the lapidary.

Various technical operations were carried out at the quarry, to detach the rock and so make it accessible, or to clean it before it could be worked by the lapidary or used by the consumer. Some stones occurred as individual pieces, and could be removed entire from earth or river, but more often suitable monoliths had to be cut away from a mass of rock or an undesirable matrix. Sometimes this difficult operation was even carried out under water by divers. For all these tasks, iron tools were used, especially chisel and mallet. In special cases, rather elaborate machinery was required. An example is the windlass, mounted on a large boat, employed to raise specimens of rock from the bed of the Grand Lake after they had been detached by divers. Another special device was the mechanical dredge (*chü hu* 車斥) used to obtain stones from the muddy bottom of a river.

It was almost always necessary to clean the specimen. Some kinds could be washed with ease, as our author takes care to point out; others must be severely brushed to remove clay or earth from the surface and deep crevices. The "Stone of Ling-pi," for instance, was scraped with iron blades, then brushed with a broom of bamboo or "yellow bud" (*huang pei* 黃薔) dipped in magnetite particles (*tz'u mo* 磁末).[51] Another cleaning tool sometimes referred to is a bamboo twig.

Even a garden stone was rarely ready for use in its raw condition. Twelfth-century connoisseurs seem not to have put a premium on "natural" stones. The Stone Catalogue tells repeatedly that the "artistry" (*ch'iao* 巧) of the specimen must be enhanced by human hands and metal tools. At a minimum, pieces must be cut level on the bottom to give them stability when set on a taboret, or they must be dressed to fit into a larger composition of rocks. The minimal lapidary work required a variety of tools: chisels, gouges, mills, and grinders of ambiguous construction (as far as Tu Wan is concerned). We may surmise from sources other than our catalogue that a variety of abrasives, such as quartz sand and garnet, were employed, but Tu Wan mentions only one, a powdered steatite used to impart a high gloss. Our author does, however, sometimes state that certain stones are too hard or tough to permit shaping.

Esthetically imperfect stones were ordinarily improved, as the text informs us, by cementing suitable fragments to their sur-

---

[51] Yü p'ien says simply "name of an herb." Its identity is now lost. Sirén (Gardens, p. 26), takes the phrase t'zu mo 磁末 to refer to powdered porcelain, since tz'u 磁 is a popular substitute for tz'u 瓷 . But neither context nor technology require this translation.

faces. Indeed, it was not an uncommon practice to attach pieces
of entirely different minerals to a miniature mountain in order
to suggest the appearance of "clouds and vapors, withered trees,
and fantastic stones tilted sidewise." Such constructions were
echoed in the *chinoiserie* of the eighteenth century: the grotto
of Alexander Pope at Twickenham was ". . . lined with a sort
of imitation tufa in which masses of more or less rare stones,
minerals, and reflecting pieces of glass were inserted." [52]

Although specimen rocks needed shaping and polishing, it was
preferred that they look old as well, if these properties were not
mutually exclusive. An apparently unique process was reserved
for the "Stones of the Grand Lake": after specimens of this
highly honored rock had been cut to properly handsome propor-
tions, they were once more immersed in the lake, where they
remained long enough to give an aged appearance to the surface.
In this instance, at least, collectors did not favor a freshly cut
surface.

A further step, for certain varieties of stone, was to plant
flowers or shrubs in the crevices. An instance is the "Stone
of K'un-shan," which was commonly planted with irises. But
this was the province of the amateur gardener rather than the
lapidary.

Stones characterized by deeply penetrating and intercom-
municating caverns often had incense set deep within them, so
that ". . . looking at them in quietude, it was as if smoke and
clouds were issuing and sinking amid cliff and alp."

Finally, fantastic stones were set on special bases for perma-
nent display. This foundation might be another specially admirable rock, like the "Stone of Wu-k'ang," which was favored in
Chekiang for the foundations of artificial mountains. Small specimens were set on little stands or tables; some were placed in
bowls or other containers. These arrangements might take the
form of miniature gardens, and were sometimes sold commer-
cially as "bowl mountains" (*p'en shan* 盆山).

Interesting and important as these landscape stones are, we

---

[52] Sirén, *China and the Gardens of Europe*, p. 21 and plate I.

can not omit mention of the stones and minerals worked into small-scale artifacts by professional lapidaries. About two-thirds of Tu Wan's book discuss these. His accounts of such materials, in particular of the abundant quartz minerals, such as agate, chalcedony, carnelian, and related species, give a distinct impression of a flourishing industry in many parts of China, and of a trade in polished stone objects even busier than the luxury commerce in grotesque garden stones. We must regret that the name of no Cellini of this age survives: custom did not permit that shapers of ink palettes and religious statuettes should be immortalized in literature. For that matter the same anonymity was forced on the dressers of landscape stones, artists who served the cultured and the mighty. In this age an admired painter was known by name, but a sculptor was a mere laborer.

Among the fine carvings noted in the *Yün lin shih p'u* are bowls, pots and boxes of all kinds, figurines of animals, men and gods, especially Buddhist, palettes, ornamental plaques and screen slabs, paperweights, seals, incense braziers, holy talismans, rosary beads, belt hooks, gongs, foot rules, and counters for the game of *go*.

Not all manufactured objects of stone noticed by Tu Wan were made in the twelfth century: stone arrowheads, although greatly admired as relics of venerated antiquity, were no longer produced. Similarly, mineral inlays in bronze are referred to by our author, but not as things made in his own time. Among these several classes of useful objects, it was the "furniture of literary culture" (*wen chü* 文具) which had the greatest value for the gentleman of the twelfth century. Next to the landscaping stones, therefore, Tu Wan gives the greatest attention to palettes for grinding carbon-black ink. In this same category belong paperweights, often mentioned in the lapidarium. So much has already been written about inkslabs both in oriental and occidental languages, however, that no special study of them is needed here. Suffice it to mention that it is apparent from Tu Wan's pages that, after the great Mi Fu himself, Su Shih (Tung-p'o) was the outstanding amateur of stone palettes during the early part of the Sung regime.

The student of the history of material culture and technology will find many points of interest in Tu Wan's book. I note a few notable examples here; others may be found in the summary of the text itself:

(1) The use of lustrous black stones as touchstones for determining the fineness of gold.[53]

(2) White pebbles, apparently feldspar, used with lead in the manufacture of glass and paste jewelry.

(3) Gypsum stamps for printing charts, pictures, and texts.

(4) A process of "boiling" and grinding malachite fragments was used to produce pigments of varying degrees of coarseness and color, apparently a kind of levigation by flotation.

(5) In this period, *fei-ts'ui* "kingfisher feather" was a term applied to lapis-lazuli from Khotan (much later to Burmese jadeite).

(6) Jet from Szechwan was made into belt hooks and the like.

(7) Iron blades, with water and sand applied for abrasive, were used to cut thin stone slabs.

Tu Wan is usually careful to list the physical attributes of his stones. These fall into several categories: color, hardness, luster, resonance. Special features, such as veinlets of a color different from the main body, suggestive of streams or waterfalls, are also mentioned. Resonance was especially important: the stone should emit a fine note when struck, like a piece of porcelain. The best sound was "clear and high pitched" (*ch'ing yüeh* 清越). Also desirable in a garden stone was a blue or green color. Great hardness and high gloss, judging from the frequency with which these qualities are assigned to the best stones, were valued. This taste differs from the modern preference for decayed, rusty, "natural"-looking rocks. Sometimes admired attributes are not mutually compatible; so limestones and sand-

---

[53] This technique is very old in the West, going back to *ca.* 600 B.C. See R. J. Forbes, *Studies in Ancient Technology*, I (Leiden, 1955), p. 125. Probably pre-Sung instances may be found in China.

stones, which are easily eroded into odd formations, are necessarily soft and seldom glossy.

Unfortunately these descriptions are seldom adequate for reliable determination of species, unless the type of stone has some unique attribute, such as the buoyancy of pumice or the vitreosity of obsidian. Generally, however, though we may surmise a serpentine or a shale, a calcite-veined andesite or a vesicular basalt, only careful examination of the actual stone could have made certain identification possible. Nonetheless I have hazarded a few guesses.

From surviving examples of ancient stone artifacts, and from other evidence, we know that the garden stones described by Tu Wan, and those praised by literary gentlemen generally, were pieces of sedimentary rock. The showpieces of private or public gardens were, in substance, the same as the chiseled blocks employed in sculpture and architecture; that is, mainly sandstone and limestone. Two familiar examples of the monumental employment of these materials are the sandstone of Yün-kang and the limestone of Lung-men. Even ancient stone chimes, such as those found in the Shang royal tombs at An-yang, were of limestone,[54] and, in much later times, soft sedimentary rock was the ordinary raw material converted into palettes, especially under the Sung dynasty.[55] Hard igneous rocks, such as diorite, basalt, and granite, were employed for such purposes only rarely, though granite-faced pagodas were characteristic of Sung times.[56] Not only are sedimentary rocks easily worked by man,

---

[54] T. Sekino, "Recent Archaeological Investigation in China," *Archaeology*, 6 (Spring, 1953), 51. The sonorous stones of Chou were usually limestone too.

[55] Wm. Hung, "The Inkslab in Chinese Literary Tradition," in *Occasional Papers*, by the scholars, fellows and their advisers in Chinese Studies at Yenching University, No. 3 (May 7, 1940). T'ang writers preferred ceramic slabs, according to Hung. Smooth, fine-textured substances such as chalcedony and jade are really not suitable for palettes.

[56] Gustav Ecke, "Structural Features of the Stone-built Ting-pagoda; a Preliminary Study," *Monumenta Serica*, 1 (1935–1936), 256. Chinese stone tools, before the general use of bronze and iron, were often made of igneous rocks, since soft stones like limestone and sandstone will not

but they lend themselves to shaping by nature. It is no accident that the monumental statues of Lung-men and the teratoid monoliths from the Grand Lake are both limestone creations, since the latter, like most stone objects placed in fantastic garden landscapes, are examples of natural sculpture and unpremeditated architecture, touched up and enhanced by the artisan's chisel. The picturesque monolith was the idol of the cultivated gentleman.

As for the stones and minerals which were cut into smaller objects, useful or ornamental, many can be reasonably identified from Tu Wan's account, especially such quartz minerals as agate, chalcedony, and rock crystal. We also detect, with some assurance, the presence of jet, coral, alabaster, lapis-lazuli, feldspar, serpentine, limonite, and malachite in these pages. This partial list checks well against the stones and minerals identified in objects preserved in the Shōsōin treasury.[57]

Tu Wan, however, though an enthusiastic and observant amateur, was no mineralogist or geologist. Doubtless the most advanced petrology of his age, if such a term can be applied to empirical understanding, was the property of some anonymous lapidary or architect, who had no opportunity to record his observations for posterity. Moreover, the compilers of the various Sung treatises on materia medica, men like K'ou Tsung-shih, though they relied heavily on their predecessors, display much

---

retain cutting edges. But the Chinese seem generally not to have made utensils of the former in historic times—certainly not to any extent comparable to the diorite utensils of the Egyptians and their like.

[57] Various soft stones and minerals, such as talc (soapstone, steatite) and serpentine, are commonly cut into ornamental objects in China. Several of these are classed under the ambiguous name "agalmatolite," a word dear to the hearts of the authors of books on the minor arts. "Agalmatolite" has no mineralogical standing; most specimens so named seem to be pyrophyllite, though micaceous and chloritic rocks, and even such substances as weathered rhyolite, pass under this venerable title. No doubt some of the stones in Tu Wan's catalogue contain much pyrophyllite. See H. T. Lee, "A Petrographical Study of the Chinese Agalmatolites," *Bulletin*, Geological Society of China, 7, 3.4 (December, 1928), 221–232.

more understanding of the properties of minerals than does Tu Wan. Perhaps even these specialists were less well informed than the alchemists, most of whose secrets are still hidden from us.

Nonetheless, the reader's attention is drawn to one point of geological interest for which our author deserves some credit, a theory of fossils. (See No. 43, pp. 67ff.) Other than this, he makes no important geological generalizations or explanations, excepting frequent references to the creation of strange rock forms and smooth beach pebbles by erosion under wind and water. Usually, however, he takes pains to ascribe such explanations to the native artisans, disdaining to commit himself on such minor matters. In the main he relies on ancient tradition for his geological views, as when he (correctly) observes the paragenesis of malachite and copper by action of "vapors." Even opinions which purport to have an empirical basis, though they appear seldom, are essentially folkloristic, as when Tu Wan records his conviction that stalactites in the form of animals and vegetables are actually petrifactions of those things. Yet the true origin of such prodigies had been known at least several centuries before his time.[58]

It is only natural that Tu Wan should classify certain organic substances, like jet and coral, among the stones.

---

[58] *Yu yang tsa tsu* (*hsü chi*), 2, 12a (*SPTK* ed.), written in the ninth century, tells of stalagmites forming under the drip from the roof of a grotto, a process observed by revisiting the cave after a period of years.

A GROUP OF THE "EIGHTEEN LEARNED GENTLEMEN" OF
THE T'ANG DYNASTY

洲播之西相對則勝瀛也其萬

騰湯若虯龍出虎陸應其狀口

容巧態莫能具備妙而言之小

延觀繪繚素耶以四韻紀之

彼美蜿蜒鷟若龍旋洑然蔦階獨樓雄

雲凝好色來相賞水潤清輝火不同

常帶暝煙疑振蕩每乘宵焰祗疼若

故憑彩筆朝摸逼岔切洪毛鳥舸

御製仙臺詩卷一廿

AUSPICIOUS DRAGON STONE

A GROUP OF THE "EIGHTEEN LEARNED GENTLEMEN" OF
THE T'ANG DYNASTY

FIVE

Language of the Catalogue

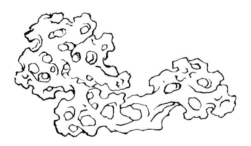

The Stone Catalogue of Cloudy Forest is written in a rather
commonplace, mannered prose. Parallelism is a frequent device,
and binomial "compounds" of various linguistic status are
abundant, more so than in ordinary narrative or descriptive
prose. There are echoes of the "rhapsody," rather subdued and
stiffened. Sometimes I am reminded of the language used by
Chiang Yen (fifth century) in his elegant "Rhapsody on Hollow
Verditer" (*K'ung ch'ing fu*), words like

> in rugged tor and layered stone,
> in tortoise hole and dragon wall;
> where silk-white cliffs shape clouds,
> with carmine sands like shoals.

But the sound is deadened, and Tu Wan's style shows no particular imaginativeness or invention. Despite this, a few remarks on its dominant features may be of interest.

The binomial expressions of the Catalogue may conveniently be divided into three classes:

(1) *Pleonasms*, including both tautologies and approximate synonyms. These are very common. Often they are entirely stylistic, as when a predication of two syllables is wanted to balance a subject of the same construction. In other cases, they belong to the class of expressions, so characteristic of Chinese, which name a pair of members of a class, sometimes the polar members, to denote members of that class collectively, or any single unspecified or unknown member of the class. Examples follow, each of them a commonly repeated term:

feng luan 峰巒 "peaks and tors" (of garden rocks resembling mountain ranges).

ch'an yen 巉岩 "craggy and precipitous" (of the same).

ch'ien k'ung 甽空 "recessed and hollowed" (of garden rocks with many cavities).

jung chieh 融結 "fused and knotted" (of stones of interesting shape, which occur, as it were, in fused groups).

wan k'uang 頑礦 "crude and coarse" (of rough-textured and dull rocks, whose constituent minerals are rather distinct; not smooth or glossy).

chi an 几案 "taboret or table" (any small stand for displaying objects of esthetic appreciation).

Many expressions of this and similar types have alternates of slightly different nuance. Consider the following, all used of landscape rocks:

ch'iao pa 峭拔 "jaggedly upthrust"
hsiu pa 秀拔 "bountifully upthrust"
sung pa 聳拔 "boldly upthrust"

(2) *Rhyming and alliterative binoms*, bisyllabic gestalt words composed of two bound constituents. These include the following very common expressions:

wan-chuan   宛轉   "tortuous; sinuous" (of garden rocks with contorted and hollowed surfaces).

ling-lung   玲瓏   "foraminate" (pierced with many holes). Cf. Chou Mi, *Kuei hsin tsa shih ch'ien chi* (*Hsüeh chin t'ao yüan* ed.), 10b-11a: "Ling-lung Mountain is on the shady side of Mount Pien; it is recessed and hollowed, singular and lofty;" a poem quoted just after this passage has, "Scooped out, opened up, and chaotic, making a *ling-lung* [appearance]." In this usage, *ling-lung* means "looking like carved openwork."

pan- po   斑剝   "dappled" [*pwan-påk], of maculated rocks; (an alliterative variant of the next, which is a rhyming binom).

pan-lan   斑斕   "dappled" [*pwan-lan].

(3) *Clichés*, essentially non-pleonastic stereotyped expressions:

yüan lin   園林   "garden grove" (a wooded natural garden).

ch'i ch'iao   奇巧   "singular and artistic" (oddly formed, as if shaped by cunning hands; high praise for a fantastic garden rock).

shua szu   刷絲   "brushed threads" (seemingly brushed with filiform striations; used especially of agate).

shuan tao   涮道   "scoured path" (*shuan* is a rare word in the literary language. The dictionary definition is "rinse." The phrase seems to mean a depressed channel, apparently scoured out by running water).

A few words of special technical usage in the Stone Catalogue are worth mentioning:

shih   勢   "contour" (the shape of a rock, especially when described as similar to another object: "having the contours of . . .").

chih   質   "substance" (qualities related to mass, hardness, and texture, exclusive of color, luster, and resonance).

tsao   燥   "coarse; gritty" (the dictionary meaning of this word is "dry; parched," but throughout this text it connotes "crumbly, friable, brittle, porous, etc.," and often appears in semipleonastic expressions like *tsao k'o*   燥渴   "porous and thirsty" [i.e., permeable]; *k'u tsao*   枯燥   "rotten and crumbly" [i.e., very brittle]; *k'uang tsao*   礦燥   "coarse and gritty" [i.e., of sandy texture]; *juan tsao*   輭燥   "soft and brittle" [i.e., easily broken]; *ts'u tsao* 麁燥 "crude and coarse" [i.e., rough of surface]).[59]

ch'ing 青 "blue" (in lapidary writing *ch'ing* is clearly distinguished from *lü* 綠 , roughly as "blue" and "green" in English, and I have so translated them). An example is in Tu Wan's description of "Stone of Shao," which is probably malachite. This mineral is usually deep green (*shen lü* 深綠), but sometimes is "blue and green conjoined" (*ch'ing lü hsiang chien* 青綠相兼), owing to inclusions of azurite in the malachite (both are copper carbonates). This plain writing differs from ancient usage. The literary language abounds in clichés containing the word *ch'ing* in reference to green things. This is true, for instance, of mineral names used by pharmacological writers, who tend to avoid new-fangled terms containing the word *lü*. In such phrases, I translate *ch'ing* by "verditer" or "bice" which, in English usage, refer to blue and green pigments and colors alike. Hence Chinese *lü ch'ing* is precisely analogous to our "green verditer," a name of malachite.

The names of two stones contain binomial expressions having *tzu* 子 "child; seed; etc." as the second element, where *tzu* seems to be a meaningless noun suffix of diminutive origin, as in modern Mandarin dialect. These are *po-tzu* 栢子 "thuja" and *lo-tzu* 螺子 "gastropod; snail." In standard literary usage *po tzu* 栢子 means "thuja seed," to be compared with *sung tzu* 松子 "pine seed." Since these expressions occur only in the names of stones discussed in Tu Wan's catalogue, it may be that they register current vernacular names, written down as heard. The term *mao-erh* 猫兒 "cat" also appears in the name of a stone mentioned in passing.

In general, in naming his stones, Tu Wan avoids old literary and classical mineral names. Most of these had, by the twelfth century, lost all exact reference, although remaining current in

---

[59] Despite these many "compounds," *tsao* 燥 is a literary "free" form, as we see from such clauses as *ch'i chih p'o tsao* 其質頗燥 and *shih p'o fa mo shao tsao* 石頗發墨稍燥 . Similar is *jun* 潤 "lustrous," despite *kuang jun* 光潤 , *ch'ing jun* 清潤 , *wen jun* 溫潤 , etc.

the language of poetry and other imaginative writing. Instances
are *ch'iung* 瓊 and *yao* 瑤 . Tu Wan had no clear idea
about the meaning of such fancy terms; no more did any
of his contemporaries. But it would have been normal for a
Chinese writer of "Confucian" persuasion to have shown an
interest in the origin of these words, attempting to relate them
to known minerals, as Pliny sought to find modern identities for
old names. But Tu Wan was little concerned with philology and
etymology. Indeed all his fine literary allusions, like his language,
have a rather unoriginal genteel flavor, as if he were the son of
a rich tradesman, or (as he was) the self-conscious descendant
of a distinguished poet. His interest in stones is genuine; his
enthusiasm for language and history is negligible. The names he
gives his stones are mostly of the type "Stone of X," where X is
the name of the locality where it is found. This practice, however, is not dissimilar from that which produced some classical
mineral names of toponymic origin in the West, however un-
recognizable they have become in modern English—names like
"agate," "chalcedony," and "turquoise," not to mention a host
of modern words such as "Iceland spar," "vesuvianite," and
"calaverite." Only a few names used by Tu Wan describe the
appearance of the stone. Such are *chung ju shih* 鐘乳石 , *hung
szu shih* 紅絲石 , and *shih sun* 石筍 , comparable to
our "carnelian," "prase," and "lapis-lazuli." Stones named for
their peculiar virtues, like "amethyst," "asbestos," and "chryso-
colla" do not appear at all in his catalogue. Ancient names of
uncertain etymology are, of course, very rare. *Ma-nao* 瑪瑙
and *lang-kan* 琅玕 are the only ones.[60]

---

[60] I do not rule out the possibility that the usual etymology of *ma-nao*,
"horse brain," is correct. *Shan-hu* "coral" occurs in the text, but not as
one of the stones to which Tu Wan devotes an article. But this word,
like *ma-nao*, and apparently *lang-kan*, were live colloquial words. Since
the Sung dynasty, *lang-kan* has joined *ch'iung* 瓊 and *yao* 瑤 and
many others in the limbo of enigmatic archaisms of politely pleasant or
poetic usage.

SIX

Synopsis and Commentary

The 114 articles of the *Ssu-pu ts'ung-k'an* edition of the Stone Catalogue of Cloudy Forest are summarized in the following pages. Although I have tried to include everything important and interesting, the manner of selection was necessarily subjective. Localities are identified with reference to the modern Chinese provinces in square brackets. My own comments and glosses follow each article, separated by two lines of space. To avoid the appearance of excessive pedantry, I have not pointed out variant readings from the several editions, or (with a few exceptions) my own emendations.[61]

---

[61] It was originally my intention to make a complete translation of the *Yün lin shih p'u*, but as the work progressed, the absence of style, imagination, or original thought, made the prospect of carrying through this considerable undertaking very unpalatable. Moreover, the constant repetition of stock phrases would have made the end result no more interesting than the summaries I present here, while occupying a great deal more space.

THE STONE CATALOGUE OF CLOUDY FOREST
Contents

1. Stone of Ling-pi (*Ling-pi shih*) 靈壁石

2. Stone of Ch'ing-*chou* (*Ch'ing-chou shih*) 青州石

3. Stone of Lin-lü (*Lin-lü shih*) 林慮石

4. Stone of the Grand Lake in P'ing-chiang-*fu* (*P'ing-chiang-fu T'ai hu shih*) 平江府太湖石

5. Stone of Wu-wei-*chün* (*Wu-wei-chün shih*) 無為軍石

6. Stone of Lin-an (*Lin-an shih*) 臨安石

7. Stone of Wu-k'ang in Hu-*chou* (*Hu-chou Wu-k'ang shih*) 湖州武康石

8. Stone of K'un-shan (*K'un-shan shih*) 崑山石

9. Stone of Chiang-hua (*Chiang-hua shih*) 江華石

10. Stone of Ch'ang-shan (*Ch'ang-shan shih*) 常山石

11. Stone of K'ai-hua (*K'ai-hua shih*) 開化石

12. Stone of Li-*chou* (*Li-chou shih*) 澧州石

13. Stone of Ying (*Ying shih*) 英石

14. Stone of Chiang-chou (*Chiang-chou shih*) 江州石

15. Stone of Yüan (*Yüan shih*) 袁石

16. Stone of P'ing-ch'üan (*P'ing-ch'üan shih*) 平泉石

17. Stone of Yen-*chou* (*Yen-chou shih*) 兗州石

18. Stone of Yung-k'ang (*Yung-k'ang shih*) 永康石

19. Serried Insignia Stones (*P'ai ya shih*) 排牙石

20. Quality Stones (*P'in shih*) 品石

21. Stone of Yung-*chou* (*Yung-chou shih*) 永州石

22. Stone Bamboo-shoots (*Shih sun*) 石筍

23. Stone of Hsi-ch'ing (*Hsi-ch'ing shih*) 襲慶石

24. Stone of Mount I (*I shan shih*) 嶧山石

25. Stone of Lei-yang (*Lei-yang shih*) 耒陽石

26. Stone of Hsiang-yang (*Hsiang-yang shih*) 襄陽石

27. Stone of Chen-chiang (*Chen-chiang shih*) 鎮江石

28. Stone of Ch'ing-ch'i (*Ch'ing-ch'i shih*) 清溪石

29. Stone of Hsing (*Hsing shih*) 邢石

30. Stone of Ch'ou-ch'ih (*Ch'ou-ch'ih shih*) 仇池石

31. Stone of the Torrent of Yüan (*Yüan ch'i shih*) 袁溪石

32. Stone of Mount Pien (*Pien shan shih*) 卞山石

33. Stone of Han-pi (*Han-pi shih*) 涵碧石

34. Stone of Chi-*chou* (*Chi-chou shih*) 吉州石

35. Stone of Ch'üan-*chou* (*Ch'üan-chou shih*) 全州石

36. Stone of Lord Ho (*Ho chün shih*) 何君石

37. Stone of the Turbid Tarn (*Cho t'an shih*) 濁潭石

38. Stone of the Vast Cliff (*Hung yen shih*) 洪岩石

39. Stone of Shao (*Shao shih*) 韶石

40. Stone of Yüan-*chou* (*Yüan-chou shih*) 袁州石

41. Stone of P'ing Hsiang (*P'ing-hsiang shih*) 萍鄉石

42. Stone of Hsiu-k'ou (*Hsiu-k'ou shih*) 修口石

43. Fish and Dragon Stones (*Yü lung shih*) 魚龍石

44. Stone of Lai (*Lai shih*) 萊石

45. Stone of Kuo (*Kuo shih*) 虢石

46. Stone of Chieh (*Chieh shih*) 階石

47. Stone of Teng-*chou* (*Teng-chou shih*) 登州石

48. Pines Transformed to Stone (*Sung hua shih*) 松化石

49. Heart-pierced Stones (*Ch'uan hsin shih*) 穿心石

50. Stones of the Lo River (*Lo ho shih*) 洛河石

51. Stone Swallows of Ling-ling (*Ling-ling shih yen*) 零陵石燕

52. Stone of Hsiang-chou (*Hsiang-chou shih*) 相州石

53. Stone of Western Shu (*Hsi Shu shih*) 西蜀石

54. Agate Stone (*Ma-nao shih*) 瑪瑙石

55. Stone of Feng-hua (*Feng-hua shih*) 奉化石

56. Stone of Chi-chou (*Chi-chou shih*) 吉州石

57. Stone of Wu-yüan (*Wu-yüan shih*) 婺源石

58. Stone of T'ung-yüan (*T'ung-yüan shih*) 通遠石

59. Stone of Lu-ho (*Lu-ho shih*) 六合石

60. Stone of Lan-chou (*Lan-chou shih*) 蘭州石

61. Stone of Tzu-chou (*Tzu-chou shih*) 淄州石

62. Stone of Ting-chou (*Ting-chou shih*) 鼎州石

63. Purple Gold Stone (*Tzu chin shih*) 紫金石

64. Stone of Chiang-chou (*Chiang-chou shih*) 絳州石

65. Stone of Ch'en-chou (*Ch'en-chou shih*) 長州石

66. Arrow Barb Stones (*Chien tsu shih*) 箭鏃石

67. Stone of Shang-yu (*Shang-yu shih*) 上猶石

68. Snail Stones (*Lo-tzu shih*) 螺子石

69. Thuja Agate Stone (*Po-tzu ma-nao shih*) 栢子瑪瑙石

70. Precious Flower Stone (*Pao hua shih*) 寶華石

71. Stone of Shih-*chou* (*Shih-chou shih*) 石州石

72. Stone of Kung (*Kung shih*) 螯石

73. Stone of Yen Mountains (*Yen shan shih*) 燕山石

74. Stone of Shao (*Shao shih*) 韶石

75. Peach Flower Stone (*T'ao hua shih*) 桃花石

76. Stone of Tuan (*Tuan shih*) 端石

77. Stone of Hsiao-Hsiang (*Hsiao-Hsiang shih*) 小湘石

78. Stone of the Office of the White Horse (*Po ma szu shih*) 白馬寺石

79. Stone of Mi (*Mi shih*) 密石

80. Stone of Square Mountain (*Fang shan shih*) 方山石

81. Parrot Stone (*Ying-wu shih*) 鸚鵡石

82. Pink Thread Stone (*Hung szu shih*) 紅絲石

83. Stone Green (*Shih lü*) 石綠

84. Stone of Wu-wei (*Wu-wei shih*) 無為石

85. Stone of Szu-*chou* (*Szu-chou shih*) 泗州石

86. Arsenical Stone (*Yü shih*) 礜石

87. Stone of Chin-hua (*Chin-hua shih*) 金華石

88. Stone of Sung-tzu (*Sung-tzu shih*) 松滋石

89. Bodhisattva Stone (*P'u-sa shih*) 菩薩石

90. Stone of Khotan (*Yü-t'ien shih*) 于闐石

91. Stone of Huang-*chou* (*Huang-chou shih*) 黃州石

92. Stone of Hua-yen (*Hua-yen shih*) 華嚴石

93. Stone of Chien-*chou* (*Chien-chou shih*) 建州石

94. Stone of Ju-*chou* (*Ju-chou shih*) 汝州石

95. Bell Teat Stone (*Chung-ju shih*) 鐘乳石

96. Rice Stones (*Fan shih*) 飯石

97. Carbon Stone (*Mo shih*) 墨石

98. Stone of Nan-chien (*Nan-chien shih*) 南劍石

99.   Stone Mirror (*Shih ching*)   石鏡

100.   *Lang-kan* Stone (*Lang-kan shih*)   琅玕石

101.   Cabbage Leaf Stone (*Ts'ai yeh shih*)   菜葉石

102.   Stone of Ts'ang-*chou* (*Ts'ang-chou shih*)   滄州石

103.   Stone of Fang-ch'eng (*Fang-ch'eng shih*)   方城石

104.   Stone of Teng-*chou* (*Teng-chou shih*)   登州石

105.   Stone of Yü-shan (*Yü-shan shih*)   玉山石

106.   Snowy Wave Stone (*Hsüeh lang shih*)   雪浪石

107.   Stone of Hang (*Hang shih*)   杭石

108.   Stone of the Great T'o (*Ta T'o shih*)   大沱石

109.   Stone of Ch'ing-*chou* (*Ch'ing-chou shih*)   青州石

110.   Dragon Fang Stones (*Lung ya shih*)   龍牙石

111.   Stone Go "Men" (*Shih ch'i tzu*)   石棋子

112.   Stone of Fen-i (*Fen-i shih*)   分宜石

113.   Bell Teat Stone (*Chung ju shih*)   鐘乳石

114.   Stone of Fou-kuang (*Fou-kuang shih*)   浮光石

THE STONE CATALOGUE OF CLOUDY FOREST

1. *Stone of Ling-pi* (Lithophone Mountain, Ling-pi-hsien, Su-*chou* [N. Anhwei])

   More than one variety, but some are very large, of great elegance, in the shapes of natural objects, such as ". . . clouds and vapors, sun and moon, or the figure of the Buddha; some exhibit the spectacle of the four seasons." Others make rugged mountains, ". . . with peaks and tors, craggy and precipitous, perforated and cavernous." Recently, the Chang family had a notable collection of specimens up to twenty feet high. Some are surely the "floating lithophones at the shores of Szu" alluded to in the *Shu ching*.

This is the most celebrated of garden stones, next to the variety from Grand Lake. The original of the "floating lithophone" of the "Tribute of Yü" is unknown, though it is easy to guess at pumice or scoria. In different ages, different stones from this region were thought to correspond to the classic name, which continued to occupy an important if hazy dignity in educated opinion. There is a curious tale of the sixth century, which tells of a woman who brought home a brightly colored stone (clearly neither that of the *Shu ching* nor that of the *Yün lin shih p'u*) from the banks of the Szu River; that same night she dreamed of the visit of a divine being who told her that the stone was the sperm (or seed, *ching* 精) of the famous floating stone chimes. (Cf. the traditional belief in the genesis of minerals from their seeds, as copper from azurite.) The apparition stated, moreover, that if she cherished this treasure, she would bear a fine son, as indeed she did. She named her boy Lin 琳 , with the byname Chi-min 季珉 , using refined and classical petronyms of uncertain reference (*Pei shih*, 66, 2957b, Biography of Kao Lin). Whatever the reliability of stories like this, the hope that the true lithophonic material might be discovered had not disappeared by Sung times. Feverishly trying to cut the formal court music to a truly classic pattern, in A.D. 966 the officials in charge of the imperial orchestras had the local magistrates institute a search for the sonorous stones along the Szu River, in order that perfect chimes might at last be achieved (*Sung shih*, 126, 4748d). It is not reported that the search was successful; indeed we may be reasonably sure that it was not, since the project was revived in A.D. 1110, but regretfully rejected, almost in the same breath, as unlikely of consummation (*Sung shih*, 129, 4791d). Yet the *Ko ku yao lun* (compiled by Ts'ao Chao in the fourteenth century, expanded by Wang Tso in the fifteenth; TSCC ed., 7,147) states that in the early years of the Ming, chimes made of ashy white Ling-pi Stone were presented to the Confucian Temple in each major city, and *An-hui t'ung chih* (1877 ed., 85, 12a), states that stones from this place are (were?) used for ceremonial chimes at the court. The private gardens of the Chang family at Ling-pi, near the Pien River, were celebrated by Su Tung-p'o in his essay, "Record of the Garden Kiosk of the Chang Clan at Ling-pi," written in A.D. 1079. The builder of the garden ". . . took fantastic stones from the mountains and made precipices of them," by the Kiosk of the Bank of Lotuses. Here were raised a great variety of trees, flowering shrubs, vegetables, and fish. See *Ching chin Tung-p'o wen chi shih lüeh* (hereafter referred to as *Tung-p'o*), 49, 3a-4a; *An-hui t'ung chih*, 50, 16a.

2. *Stone of Ch'ing-chou* (Ch'ing-chou [C. Shantung])
    A rather soft garden stone, zoned with purple, remarkable for abundance of perforations.

Mi Fu mentions this also among the palette stones in his *Yen shih*.

3. *Stone of Lin-lü* (Chiao-k'ou, Lin-lü-*hsien*, Hsiang[a]-*chou* [N. Honan])
   The best specimens are deep green, resembling natural objects, or chains of contorted pinnacles. Formerly the most beautiful, only a few inches high, were sent to the treasury. More than ten varieties of these latter were distinguished, including "Indigo Barrier" (*lan kuan* 藍關), "Grass-green Serpent" (*ts'ang ch'iu* 蒼虯), and "Grottoed Heaven" (*tung t'ien* 洞天). A black variety was discovered by a Taoist geomancer in the period A.D. 1102–1106.

The "treasury" is the repository (*nei fu* 內府) for Hui Tsung's objects of art. For many more examples of the splendid names bestowed by the sovereign on his stones, names like "Bouquet of Jades" (*yün yü* 蘊玉), "Dancing Sylph" (*wu hsien* 舞仙), "Amassed Snow" (*chi hsüeh* 積雪), see the *Hsüan ho shih p'u*, ascribed to "Tsu-k'ao," in *Ming ch'ao pen Shuo fu*. A stone catalogue of the seventeenth century, the *Su yüan shih p'u* of Lin Yu-lin, contains woodcut representations of sixty-five stones, including those just named, purporting to be those of the Hsüan ho Collection. I cannot guess how these pictures were made five centuries after Hui Tsung's time. Some of them are reproduced as vignettes in this book.

4. *Stone of the Grand Lake in P'ing-chiang-fu* (Tung-t'ing Lake, P'ing-chiang-*fu* [S. Kiangsu])
   Huge specimens, up to fifty feet high, with a color range from white through pale blue to blue-black, their surfaces textured in netlike relief, are hauled out of the lake. The most desirable have tortuous, rugged contours, and abundant hollows. Small surface cavities are called "arbalest pellet nests" (*t'an*

tzu wo 彈子窩); these are thought to have been
made by wind and water. Reshaped specimens are
aged by replacing them in the lake. Some are quite
small, and displayed on stands.

Tung-t'ing Lake, "Lake of the Grotto Court," is not here the
great lake in Hunan Province, but is another name for the
"Grand Lake" hard by Soochow. These great limestone blocks
are the most famous of all garden stones, first given renown in
prose and verse by Po Chü-i. In later times they were revered as
stunning antiquities, and were already very rare in the seventeenth century. See O. Sirén, *Gardens of China* (New York,
1949), p. 25, quoting *Yüan yeh*. Not only were these stones re-
worked to improve their appearance, but they were sometimes
artificially darkened with smoke, or dyed to imitate the color of
the Ling-pi Stones. See Chao Hsi-hu, *Tung t'ien ch'ing lu* (*Ming
ch'ao pen Shuo fu*), pp. 31a-b. Su Tung-p'o wrote a poem on
small water-polished pebbles, which he kept in a dish for plant-
ing sweet-flags. He says that the local name for these is "arbalest
pellet eddies" (*t'an tzu wo*   彈子渦   ). *Wo* "eddies" is cog-
nate to *wo* "nests," both referring to cuplike depressions. In Su's
usage, however, the term applies to an object which would fit in
such a cavity. I find no dictionary authority for this meaning.
See *Tung-p'o*, 8, 21a.

5. *Stone of Wu-wei-chün* (Wu-wei-chün [S.C. Anhwei])
    Black aggregates of peaks. A beautiful example
    which once belonged to the Chang Clan was pro-
    cured by Wei Yang-yü. It was named "Stone of a
    Thousand Pinnacles." Another such belonged to
    Mi Fu. Few are mined and they are hard to obtain.

6. *Stone of Lin-an* (Lin-an-*hsien*, Hang-*chou* [Che-
    kiang])
    Fantastic shapes of various shades of blue, up to

ten feet high. An excellent piece, acquired by a priest at great cost, was kept at the "Close of a Thousand *Ch'ing*" in Ch'ien-t'ang. There was a single loquat planted in a crevice of this stone. Because of the dew which collected on it, it was named "Pearl Stone" (*kuei shih* 瑰石).

7. *Stone of Wu-k'ang in Hu-chou* (Wu-k'ang-*hsien*, Hu-*chou* [N. Chekiang])
Flat, layered, without peaks, but much perforated. Adaptable to bases of artificial mountains.

8. *Stone of K'un-shan* (K'un-shan-*hsien*, P'ing-chiang-*fu* [S. Kiangsu]) .
A white stone, rugged and perforated, without sharp peaks. Recently a stone of identical appearance was found in Hang-*chou*. It is sometimes planted with shrubs and flowers; some are put in containers.

9. *Stone of Chiang-hua* (Chiang-hua-*hsien* and Yung-ning-*hsien*, Tao-*chou* [S. Hunan])
The Chiang-hua variety is usually not interesting. The blue-black specimens from Yung-ning show a great variety of curious forms, especially mountain landscapes with white waterfalls and streams.

10. *Stone of Ch'ang-shan* (Torrent of Szu, also called Flood of Stones or Empty Precinct, Ch'ang-shan-*hsien*, Ch'ü-*chou* [S.W. Chekiang])
A bluish stone, sometimes veined. Never larger than a few feet, it occurs in a great variety of extraordinary eroded shapes. Some have very slender

spires, called "stone bamboo-shoots" (*shih sun* 石筍).

11. *Stone of K'ai-hua* (Dragon Mountain and in water at Turtle Shoal nearby, K'ai-hua-*hsien*, Ch'ü-*chou* [S.W. Chekiang])
Rough, with rows of peaks, but not sharply jagged.

12. *Stone of Li-chou* (Li-*chou* [N. Hunan])
Small pieces of bluish-white stone, with networks of white veins, in various strange shapes. These are not appreciated by the natives, but traveling gentlemen take them home to build up simulacra of Mount Yen-tang in Chekiang.

13. *Stone of Ying* (Between Han-kuang-*hsien* and Chen-yang-*hsien*, Ying-*chou* [Kwangtung])
Variously colored rock, with peaks and hollows, taken out of a river. A white variety is sharply spired and lustrous as a mirror. Merchants profit little from these stones, because of the remoteness of their source, though tales are told of fantastic prices paid for them. Su Tung-p'o had a pair, one green, one white, which he named for Mount Ch'ou-ch'ih. My fellow townsmen Wang K'uo-fu had a collection of them.

Su kept his stones on a stand, in a dish of water. He refers to this pair in more than one poem. See *Tung-p'o*, 8, 22b; 8, 32b; and 8, 33a-b. Mount Ch'ou-ch'ih is in Kansu. It had a special place in Taoist mythology, one reason for its appeal to the Taoist poet. See Stein, *Jardins*, pp. 61–62, for details.

14. *Stone of Chiang-chou* (Hu-k'ou-*hsien*, Chiang-*chou*
[N. Kiangsi])
Several different kinds taken from the river and
along the shore. A notable species, finely striated,
comes in flat pieces, pierced through with holes,
". . . with the aspect of a wooden board, seemingly gouged and incised by sharp knives." This
kind is often improved by cementing pieces of
other rock to it. Li Cheng-ch'en of Hu-k'ou had
a collection of these; one of them was praised by
Su Tung-p'o as "Nine Flowers within a Pot."
"Vertical" varieties of this stone are made into
tasteless miniature gardens, called "bowl mountains," with the pieces glued in a formal array, like
offerings on a Buddhist altar. These are sold by
the natives.

"Nine Flowers" is the name of a famous nine-peaked mountain in Anhwei. The preface to Su's poem "Nine Flowers within
a Pot" tells how the poet tried to purchase this stone from Li
Cheng-ch'en for "a hundred in gold," to match his Ch'ou-ch'ih
stones. (See Stone of Ying, above.) The deal was never con-
summated, because Su was transferred to the South. In the poem
he describes the rock as prase-colored (*pi* 碧) and foraminate.
In the preface to another poem he tells how he visited Hu-k'ou
again after the lapse of eight years, only to find that the mar-
vellous stone had been acquired by another collector. Stein,
(*Jardins*, pp. 45–63), discusses the important notion of the uni-
verse in the image of a calabash-pot, exemplified here.

15. *Stone of Yüan* (Village of Disordered Stones, near
Wan-tsai-*hsien*, Yüan-*chou* [W. Kiangsi])
Corrugate and peaked, with plants growing natu-

rally in fissures like dense groves of trees. Unfortunately they are not widely known.

16. *Stone of P'ing ch'üan*   (Kuan-*chung* [Shensi])

Li Te-yü cut the words "Possessing the Way" (*yu tao* 有道) on rare stones in a garden of his villa at P'ing-ch'üan. Recently I saw such a stone, with the same words engraved on it, at the residence of Tu Ch'in-i in Ying-ch'ang. It had two peaks, but otherwise lacked projections or holes. It was brightly polished, hard, and resonant.

Ying-ch'ang is east of Loyang. Li Te-yü described his garden stones in his essay *P'ing-ch'üan shan chü ts'ao mu chi.* (See *Li Wei-kung Hui-ch'ang i p'in chi* [TSCC ed.], p. 232.) The words of the great statesman are: "Fantastic stones of the Passes of T'ai[a] [Mt. T'ai in Shantung] and of the Eight Lords [Mountain of the Eight Lords in Anhwei], from the sheer rapids of the Shaman's Gorge [on the Yangtze River in Hupeh], and water stones of the Terrace of Lang-yeh [raised by Ch'in Shih Huang Ti on Lang-yeh Mountain in southern Shantung], I spread at the side of a clear watercourse. Stones with sylph-man's [*hsien* 仙] tracks and tracks of deer, I arrayed at the front of Buddha's couch." Apparently most of these marvels were looted and dispersed during the Huang Ch'ao rebellion and the troubles of the tenth century, but alleged specimens continued to appear from time to time. An instance other than the one described by Tu Wan is the "Stone of Li Te-yü," to which I referred above in my account of some corrupt versions of Tu Wan's text. This latter stone was his "Stone which Sobers from Wine" (*hsing chiu shih* 醒酒石). Supposedly, after a long and varied history it was finally lodged at the Sung imperial palace during the period A.D. 1094–1097. Information on the fate of such garden treasures may be found in Yeh Meng-te's postface to Li Te-yü's essay (in the *T'ang tai ts'ung shu* edition), in *Wu Tai shih*, 45, 4438d (Biography of Chang Ch'üan-i), and in Li

Ko-fei, *Lo-lang ming-yüan chi* (Han fen lou ed. of *Shuo fu*, 26, 4a-11b).

17. *Stone of Yen-chou* (Yen-*chou* [W. Shantung])
    A tough stone, called "chestnut jade" (*li yü* 栗玉) for its brown color. Unperforated, but has cliffs and peaks. Much valued by artisans, since it can be ground, though with difficulty, to make utensils. It closely resembles a "chestnut jade" produced by the "Northern Caitiffs" (*po lu* 北虜).

Mi Fu, in his "History of Palettes," writes of a "chestnut jade" from Ch'eng-*chou*, used to make inkslabs. It is not clear whether he refers to the familiar Ch'eng-*chou* in what is now S.E. Kansu, or to the place of the same name, but little noted, created by the Khitans in Manchuria. If the latter, this would be the second variety mentioned by Tu Wan.

18. *Stone of Yung-k'ang* (Yung-k'ang-*chün*, Shu-chung [W. Szechwan])
    Ch'ien Sun-shu gave me a specimen which was flat like a board, half an inch thick, and six or seven inches wide. A steep many-peaked blue-black mountain rose from this white base. This was named "Little Plain of the River and Mountain." Sun-shu obtained it from a person who said it originated in Yung-k'ang, but none other like it has been discovered.

19. *Serried Insignia Stones* (Suburb Saluting Terrace, a mountain near Lin-an-*fu* headquarters [Chekiang])
    Jagged, perforated, kingfisher-blue stones, protruding like an array of military emblems from the

ground in a region abounding in relics of the
Ch'ien dynasty of Wu-yüeh.

YTCS, 2, 22b, lists "Serried Insignia Stones" (*p'ai ya shih*
排衙石   ) in this region; presumably they were the same. *Ya*
牙   and *ya* 衙   (analogous to the eagles of the Roman
legions) are interchangeable. Cf. the stones of Chenchiang, No.
27, below.

20. *Quality Stones* (Chien-k'ang-*fu* [S. Kiangsu])
     Here are three pieces of this greenish stone. They
     are "masculine and imposing," marked with cliffs
     and grottoes, and densely grown with bamboos
     and trees. The name "Quality Stones" (*p'in shih*
     品石) refers to incised inscriptions by notables
     of the Six Dynasties, T'ang, and Sung.

Admirable landscape stones were often inscribed with names
and texts, like the specimen from the Grand Lake of the tenth
century, which had the characters *ch'ung hsien* 寵仙   inlaid
in gold (See *Ch'ing i lu*, 2, 4a, in ed. of *Hsi yin hsüan ts'ung
shu*). I cannot tell from the description of the "Quality Stones"
whether they are the three referred to in *YTCS*, 17, 25a, said to
have been erected here in A. D. 922. If so, they were already
inscribed, and imported from elsewhere.

21. *Stone of Yung-chou* (Mountainside east of the
     magistrate's audience hall, Yung-*chou* [S. Hunan])
     A rocky hill laid bare by Huang Shu-pao, who re-
     moved quantities of soil. There are pinnacles and
     intercommunicating grottoes. On the peaks are en-
     graved texts of the T'ang period. In the water is
     a stone with the form of a tufted duck (*ch'i-ch'ih*
     鸂鶒). In the fields beyond the hill are many
     fantastic stones which provide shade for the resi-

dents. The "Kiosk of the Myriad Stones" was
founded by Yüan Tz'u-shan on the crest of the
ridge here.

Yüan Tz'u-shan is Yüan Chieh, a well-known traveling magistrate of the eighth century (See *Ming i t'ung chih*, 65, 17a-b.)
Traces of a shrine and a residence associated with him survived
in this picturesque region into late Sung times (*YTCS*, 56, 10a).
However, *YTCS*, 56, 6b, relying on a statement by Liu Tsung-
yüan, states that the kiosk was built by a T'ang civil magistrate
named Ts'ui Neng.

22. *Stone Bamboo-shoots* (1, Yellow Mountain, Chen-
     chiang-*fu* [S. Kiangsu]; 2, Shang-*chou* [S.E. Shensi];
     3, I-*chou* [Szechwan])
     Various colors and shapes; characteristically it has
     sharp spikes, with filiform patterns in low relief.

Cf. reference to these stones under "Stone of Ch'ang-shan,"
above. W. Eberhard reports various myths and legends connected with these bamboo stones. See his *Lokalkulturen*, I, 333,
383–384.

23. *Stone of Hsi-ch'ing* (Mount T'ai, Hsi-ch'ing-*fu*
     [Shantung])
     A soft rock, gray or pale blue, in bizarre hollowed
     shapes. Though readily carved, it is not prized
     by the natives.

24. *Stone of Mount I* (Mount I, Tsou-*hsien*, Hsi-
     ch'ing-*fu* [Shantung])
     Steep and cliffy, with shallow holes; indigo or
     bright blue-green. Very hard and unworkable.

25. *Stone of Lei-yang* (Lei-yang-*hsien*, Heng-*chou* [S. Hunan])
    Small stones of various color and odd shape, suitable for display on stands.

26. *Stone of Hsiang-yang* (Phoenix Mountain, near Hsiang-yang-*fu* [N. Hupeh])
    Mountain-shaped stones of no great size; not valued by the natives. Su Chung-kung had a collection mounted on stands in his home at Chen-chiang not many years ago.

Su Chung-kung, mentioned also in the next three articles, was evidently a private gentleman without political attainments, since his name is not recorded in national or local histories.

27. *Stone of Chen-chiang* (Yellow Mountain and Mount Hsien, near Chen-chiang-*fu* [S. Kiangsu])
    A glossy yellow or light-brown stone, in many freakish shapes, with penetrating holes suitable for incense. Su Chung-kung had some, including one resembling a crouching tiger and another like a tufted duck asleep. Mei Chih-sheng, the Grand Protector, called these "The Serried Insignia Stones of the Su Clansman." A "Stone Bamboo-shoot" nine feet high he called "Su's Ridgepole Beam." All these were eventually brought to the imperial palace. Mi Fu had one, in the shape of a mountain, which he used as an ink palette.

Mi Fu's "palette mountain" (*yen shan*   硯山   ) belonged originally to Li Yü, the poet-monarch of Southern T'ang (tenth century). It passed through many hands until it came to Mi

Fu, who gave it to Su Chung-kung. Unless awarded playfully, the name "Serried Insignia" may indicate that Su was a magistrate. This crown jewel, too, came finally into Hui Tsung's collection. See Chia Szu-tao (thirteenth century), *Yüeh sheng sui ch'ao* (in *Ming ch'ao pen Shuo fu*, 12, 4a-b).

28. *Stone of Ch'ing-ch'i* (near Ch'ing-ch'i-*chen*, Kuang-nan [E. Kwangtung])

    There is a white variety, and a blue variety with a fine clear note. Su Chung-kung had several specimens of this rugged picturesque rock displayed on stands. The ground in the vicinity of the quarry is noted for its blue and green color.

29. *Stone of Hsing* (mountains near T'ai-hang Range, west of Hsing-*chou* [S.W. Hopei])

    A strange, black, pinnacled stone. Called "raven stone" (*wu shih* 烏石), when used for palette manufacture. Su Chung-kung had three of these inkstones.

30. *Stone of Ch'ou-ch'ih* (Ch'ou-ch'ih, S.W. of Shao-*chou* [N. Kwangtung])

    A bizarre, peaked stone, similar to Stone of Ch'ing-ch'i.

The source of this stone is named after the famous mountain in Kansu, but remains unidentified.

31. *Stone of the Torrent of Yüan* (Yüan-*chou* [W. Kiangsi])

    Blue-black stones, steep-sided and hollowed, from a stream torrent (*ch'i* 溪). They are often

very large. The T'ang recluse Lu Chao had a specimen more than ten feet high, near his streamside
hut. He called it "Lu's Torrent Stone." Hui Tsung
proposed to take it for his palace collection, but
old inscriptions containing tabooed words were
found on it, so the project was abandoned.

Lu Chao was a native of the town of I-ch'un in the ninth
century. Encouraged by the exalted Li Te-yü, who held a temporary post there, he brought fame to his home town by taking
a "first" (*chuang yüan* 狀元) at the imperial examinations.
His studio here was a place for sight-seers even in Sung times,
as was the stone associated with his name. See YTCS, 28, 4a,
9b-10a, 10b, 11a.

32. *Stone of Mount Pien* (Mount Pien, in the range
     west of Hu-*chou* [N. Chekiang])
     Rubble scattered about the mountainside. The
     stones resemble those of Ling-pi. Yeh Shao-yün
     acquired the property and built a hall whence the
     landscape could be admired, hence the name
     "Forest of Stones." These stones bear T'ang in-
     scriptions. Northwest of Hu-*chou*, behind Phoenix
     Mountain, there are also great blue, perforated
     stones. I tried to have one carried off during the
     reign "Promulgated Accord" (A. D. 1119–1125),
     but it was too heavy to move. Some pieces still
     remain by the roadside.

Yeh Shao-yün was the famous writer Yeh Meng-te, a contemporary of Tu Wan. His study, where he spent his declining
years, was called "Forest of Stones," after the view; he took the
same names as his personal epithet. See YTCS, 4, 23b.

33. *Stone of Han-pi* (South of Yung-yang-*hsien*, Wu-*chou* [Chekiang])
    The T'ang magistrate Yü Hsing-tsung created a pool, named "Immersed in Prase" (*han pi* 涵碧), and a waterfall here. There are two stone fish in the pond. Near them is an admirable craggy rock about two feet high whose center portion is concave. Lo Chiang-tung used to come here to write in the coolness of the garden, and employed this rock as a palette. Connoisseurs visit the spot frequently, and Liu Yü-hsi wrote a poem about it.

Yü Hsing-tsung was "commandant" (*ling* 令) in Tung-yang about 825 or 826. Lo Chiang-tung was the celebrated poet Lo Yin (A. D. 833–909); he had a residence here, and a kiosk by the pool. (See *Ming i t'ung chih*, 42, 9a, 11a.) Liu Yü-hsi's poem was presented to Magistrate Yü when the latter, anxious to make this pleasance famous, gave him a picture of it. See *Liu Meng-te wen chi*, 5, 8b-9b (*SPTK*).

34. *Stone of Chi-chou* (An-fu-*hsien*,Chi- *chou* [Kiangsi)]
    Several kinds: (1) a large, rugged, glossy variety, in the mountains just east of the *hsien*; (2) strangely shaped stones at the Ancestral Shrine of the White Horse, farther east; (3) deeply pitted stones, and also mountain-shaped rocks, at the Tarn of the Buddhist Samgha, west of the *hsien*; (4) jagged, perforated rocks, some resembling creatures, by a cave in a steep cliff near Ch'ing-yün Hamlet, farther west. These stones need a higher luster to be quite beautiful.

35. *Stone of Ch'üan-chou* (Hsiang River, Ch'üan-chou [N. Kwangsi])
    Stalactitic stones in a myriad of wonderful shapes,

along both banks up stream. They are bright
blue, like the stone of Ling-pi, and beautifully
resonant. Approaching in a boat, I was able to
knock off several artistic pieces.

36. *Stone of Lord Ho* (Jade Hamper Mountain, Hsin-
kan-*hsien*, Lin-chiang-*chün* [Kiangsi])
Huge and wonderful monoliths in the vicinity of a
deep grotto where, according to tradition, once
lived a Taoist "sylph-man" named Lord Ho. There
is a stone gaming board in the grotto. Formerly
there was a cloud-like piece, translucent green,
hanging at the entrance, but this was broken off
by a native, also named Ho, who set it up in a
garden pavilion.

One thinks of the Taoist divinity Ho Hsien-ku here, but a
different immortal seems to be meant. *YTCS*, 34, 9a, calls
him Ho Tzu-hsiao. Jade Hamper Mountain is shrouded in
Taoist lore of considerable antiquity. (See *YTCS*, 34, 6a.) The
name of the modern vandal is just a curious coincidence.

37. *Stone of Turbid Tarn* (Up the Chi-pu River from
Feng-ch'eng, northeast of Kao-an-*hsien*, Yün-*chou*
[Kiangsi])
Steep-sided, perforated, greenish rocks, in the
water of the "Turbid Tarn."

For *cho* 濁 "turbid," other editions have *shu* 斵
or 孰 .

38. *Stone of the Vast Cliff* (East Mountain Hamlet,
Le-p'ing-*hsien*, Jao-*chou* [N. Kiangsi])

Take torches into a grotto at the "Vast Cliff," and
descend to a place where the roar of invisible rush-
ing water can be heard. Here are drums, bells,
chimes, a "sylph-man's canopy." Nearby are
figures of the Buddha and his arhats, all naturally
formed in the green rock of the mountain.

Another series of limestone caves. YTCS, 23, 8a, says that it
runs some 400 feet north and south, and has "rocks like halls,
like canopies, like images, like horses, exceedingly abundant."

39. *Stone of Shao* (Yellow Ox Shoal, Shao-*chou* [N.
Kwangtung])
Gray stone, with peaks and other singular features,
taken from the river bed. The color becomes
rather blue after the weathered surface has been
brushed with magnetite. Even small specimens are
interesting. The price is about the same as for
Stone of Yung-ming in Tao-*chou*.

Tao-*chou* is in southern Hunan, but Tu Wan does not mention this stone elsewhere.

40. *Stone of Yüan-chou* (near Fen-i-*hsien*, Yüan-*chou*
[W. Kiangsi])
A wild, rocky landscape, inhabited by monkeys, at
the Mountain Pass of the Five Apes, where purple
stones, polymorphous and foraminate, lie helter-
skelter. Lu Tzu-ming of Lin-chiang, a petromaniac, took many away by boat. Not far from
here is a fantastic chambered grotto, called
"Grotto of Hung and Yang," named for the two
alchemists Ko Hung and Lou Yang of the fourth
century, who are said to have stayed here. There

are stalactites and other formations in the shape of animals, grain bins, ships, and the like, as well as T'ang inscriptions. Recently a Taoist proposed to explore the whole extent of the cavern with a torch, but he was frightened by the sound of a boat being poled above his head, and fled.

There are also inscriptions of the fourth and fifth centuries in the cave. (See YTCS, 28, 8b.) Lu Tzu-ming is Lu Wan, but I have no information about him.

41.   *Stone of P'ing-hsiang* (near P'ing-hsiang-*hsien*, Yüan-*chou* [W. Kiangsi])
Stones, hanging like stalactites, hollowed into various peculiar forms, in a grotto at the place called "Stone Observatory." There are also many strange stones lying hid in the bamboo groves nearby, but the natives do not value them.

This is one of many grottoes in this region; cf. No. 40 above.

42.   *Stone of Hsiu-k'ou* (Hsiu-k'ou, Fen-ning-*hsien*, Hung-*chou* [N. Kiangsi])
Fine-grained stone with polychromatic patterns, suggesting tortoise shell, mined from deep underground. Sometimes it takes the shape of natural objects. The natives work it into vessels, and it is said to be suitable for palettes.

MIDDLE SCROLL

43.   *Fish and Dragon Stones* (Hsiang-hsiang-*hsien*, T'an-*chou* [N. Hunan])
A bluish or gray stone excavated at the top of a

mountain. It contains images of fish, which seem
to be loach and carp, as if drawn in ink, with fins
and scales plainly shown. Also there are "dragons"
of undulating shape, with fins and claws. The
natives make counterfeits of lacquer, but the genuine article can be distinguished by the fishy odor
it gives off when burned. Similar stone fish are
found at the "Stream of Fish and Dragons" in
Lung-hsi. "Surely it cannot be otherwise than that
here were marshes and meres in antiquity, and the
fish lived in their midst. But because of clogging
by landslides from the mountains, they congealed
in the soil over long years, and so came to this."
Tu Fu refers to the stone fish and dragons of
Lung-hsi in a poem.

For Tu Fu's reference to the Lung-hsi fossils, see note 28,
p. 15f. The Hunan site is called "Stone Fish Mountain" (*Hunan t'ung chih* [1885 ed.], 15, 1a; 60, 13b). It is ten or fifteen *li*
west of the *hsien*. These fossils are well known. They are described in *Shui ching chu* (SPTK), 38, 3b, as occurring in a
micaceous black rock, apparently a slate or phyllite. An almost
identical account appears in Shen Huai-yüan, *Nan Yüeh chih*
(*Wu ch'ao hsiao shuo* ed.), 1a, but the date of this book is unknown, though it may be earlier than the sixth century, when
the *Shui ching chu* was composed. Chu Hsi is usually given
credit for first announcing a credible theory of fossils (see L. C.
Goodrich in *Isis*, 34 [Summer, 1942], 25), but Tu Wan, in view
of his statement here, should be allowed the glory of priority,
as has already been shown by R. C. Rudolph. Apparently the
earliest statement about petrifaction of an ancient organic material in the earth, however, can be found in *Po wu chih* (ca. A. D.
290) and also in *Yüan chung chi* (third or fourth century). The
passages in these two books (as quoted in *T'ai p'ing yü lan*, 808,
2a) are very similar. The simplest is that of *Yüan chung chi*,
which says, "When the gum of the liquidambar is engulfed

within the earth, after a thousand years it becomes amber." For discussions of these and other notices of fossils in China, see B. Laufer, *Notes on Turquoise in the East* (Field Museum of Natural History, Publication 169, Anthropological Series, Vol. 13, No. 1, Chicago, 1913, pp. 22–24); Richard C. Rudolph, "Early Chinese References to Fossil Fish," *Isis*, 36 (October, 1946), 155; and H. T. Chang, *Lapidarium Sinicum* (*Memoirs of the Geological Survey of China*, Ser. B, No. 2 (May, 1921), pp. 229–243. H. T. Chang seems to regard most stone dragons as oddly shaped stalagmites, and he has reproduced photographs of several. Tu Wan's dragons, however, seem more likely to be fossils of some aquatic creature. We now have a full account of the history of Chinese palaeontology in Joseph Needham, *Science and Civilization in China*, 3 vols. (Cambridge University Press, 1954–1959). See Vol. III: *Mathematics and the Science of the Heavens and the Earth*, pp. 611–623, esp. pp. 599–607. Needham has pushed back the theory of cataclysmic elevations of the sea bottom to about the fourth century or earlier, but no statement as clear as Tu Wan's appears in this early literature.

44. *Stone of Lai* (Lai-*chou* [Shantung])
     Some is deep blue-black, translucent, mottled, and crisscrossed with veins; some is white. It is soft enough to be readily carved into delicately shaped vessels. It hardens in the air. Cooking vessels made of it stand much use, and are superior to those of copper and iron.

This seems likely to be a serpentine, but guesses are vain.

45. *Stone of Kuo* (Chu-yang-*hsien*, Kuo-*chou* [W. Honan])
     White enclosures in a dark violet matrix, moon-

shaped, tortoise-shaped, or toad-shaped. Local
artisans perfect these forms with chemicals and
tools. Ou-yang Hsiu wrote a poem about a screen-
tablet made of this stone, called "Stone Screen of
the Clouds and Moon." Another variety shows
mountain peaks and valleys on a pale yellow background. Small pieces are often shaped into figurines, and it is also suitable for palettes, and for
plaques displayed like paintings on taborets. The
natives say that the designs are caused by seepage
of water.

This seems to be a marble, permeated with solutions bearing
manganese oxide, or another coloring agent. Screens such as the
ones described here were simple translucent plaques set on edge
—ornaments rather than functional screens. I have not found
Ou-yang Hsiu's poem, although he wrote several on the subject
of decorative stone screens, which he admired extravagantly. In
one, "Song of the Stone Screen of the Learned Gentlemen Wu,"
he gives high praise to the artisans of Kuo.

46. *Stone of Chieh* (Chieh-*chou* [S.E. Kansu])
A soft stone, which hardens on exposure. Locally
it is cut into representations of the Buddha and
other figurines. It is burnished with powdered
soapstone to give it a high gloss. Some is ground
into beautiful hyaline slabs for palettes and screens.
The imperial court uses this stone to make talismans ("Gold Tablets and Jade Notes" [*chin ts'e
yü chien*　金冊玉簡　]) which are inscribed in
vermilion and deposited in holy spots in the mountains.

From the description, this can hardly be anything but
alabaster.

47. *Stone of Teng-chou* (Seashore at Teng-*chou* [Shan-
    tung])
    Small white pebbles, sometimes translucent. They
    resemble euryale seeds (*ch'ien shih* 芡實),
    though some are the size of cherries. The natives
    call them "arbalest pellet eddies," and say they
    are produced by the buffeting of wind and wave.

  See gloss on No. 4, "Stone of the Grand Lake," about these
"eddies." These little pebbles are called "Pearl-bead stones"
(*chu chi shih* 珠璣石) in *Shan-tung t'ung chih* (1934
ed.), 41, 1519. G. A. Stuart describes the seeds of *Euryale ferox*
as ". . . of a reddish color, mottled and veined with a whitish
marbling," and states that the Chinese compare them to fish
eyes (*Chinese Materia Medica* [Shanghai, 1911]. The description would fit water-washed adularia (moonstone).

48. *Pines Transformed to Stone* (Yung-k'ang-*hsien*,
    Wu-chou [Chekiang])
    The destruction of a pine grove by lightning and
    the consequent petrifaction of the trees was wit-
    nessed here by Ma Tzu-jan. They are broken in
    many pieces, which show the original grain of the
    wood. The natives use them for chairs, and the
    smaller fragments look well when displayed upon
    stands.

  Apparently petrified wood (changed to opal or chalcedony).
Some editions add that the ninth-century poet Lu Kuei-meng
reported petrified pines at the same place. The identity of Ma
Tzu-jan is uncertain. *YTCS*, 4, 24b, gives an anecdote about
a Taoist of this name in Hu-*chou*; I do not know if he is the
same person as the eccentric vagabond, alternately called Ma

Hsiang, of Giles, *Chinese Biographical Dictionary* No. 1487. One version of the story of the storm may be found in Tu Kuang-t'ing, *Lu i chi*, 5a-b (*Shuo fu*).

49. *Heart-pierced Stones* (in river at Hsiang^b-*chou* [N. Hupeh])

    Little blue-black pebbles, each with a hole, hence the name. The natives grope for them in the river bed each spring, as a way of divining the number of sons they will have. Recently my brother found one as large as a goose egg. It was blue, with two lines of white markings, suggesting cursive script done in ceruse. He was robbed of it by a young aristocrat. No other like it has been found.

50. *Stones of the Lo River* (in the Lo River, at the Western capital [Honan])

    Fragments of stone, usually pale blue, but some mottled in various colors. The whitest ones are used with lead and other reagents to make glass and artificial gems.

Apparently a feldspar, most likely microcline.

51. *Stone Swallows of Ling-ling* (Ling-ling-*hsien*, Yung-*chou* [S. Hunan])

    There is an old tradition that these stone birds can fly when it rains. I visited the site and saw many of them. They might break off if the rock disintegrates under rain and sun and fall to the ground, but they could not fly.

YTCS, 56, 8a, calls the site "Stone Swallow Mountain." The swallows seem to be fossil spirifers. See H. T. Chang, *Lapida-*

rium, R. C. Rudolph, "Fossil Fish," and B. E. Read and C. Pak, "A Compendium of Minerals and Stones used in Chinese Medicine from Pen Ts'ao Kang Mu; Li Shih Chen A.D. 1597," *Bulletin,* Peking Society of Natural History, 3, 2 (December, 1928), 66–67.

52. *Stone of Hsiangᵃ-chou* (The Pear Garden, north of Hsiang-*chou* [N. Honan])
     Several kinds of glossy stone found in deep water. Some are spotted as with ink. Some are dark yellow, and called "ginger pickles" (*chiang shih* 薑豉) by the natives. They can be worked into utensils or ground into paperweights; these are sold at very reasonable prices.

53. *Stone of Western Shu* (Western Shu [Szechwan])
     Bean-size stones of various colors, usually dull gray permeated with veins. They are cut into paperweights shaped like tortoises and toads. One variety is locally made, with the help of cement, into the figure of a white or red serpent coiled on the back of a maculated black tortoise. The natives call this "Stone of the Dark Warrior" (*hsüan wu shih* 玄武石).

     Hsüan wu shih means "basalt" in modern Chinese, an entirely different usage.

54. *Agate Stone* (I-tuᵃ-*hsien,* Hsia-*chou* [Hupeh])
     An elegantly veined agate, much encrusted with sand and silt which must be broken off. It is patterned with the forms of human beings, animals, and clouds. Specimens are sold in the local markets. Good agate is also found at "The Mountain

Heaped with Jewels" at Hsü-i-*hsien* and at Chao-hsin-*hsien*, both in Szu-*chou* [N. Kiangsu]. The magistrate at Chao-hsin obtained a large specimen from a peasant during the period A.D. 1111–1117. This was ground to show a coiled yellow dragon on a white background; it was taken for the imperial treasury.

Cf. Stone of Szu No. 85 below. By Sung times at least, as is apparent from the present text, the word *ma-nao* denoted all kinds of cryptocrystalline quartz equally, including chalcedony, agate, carnelian, onyx, chrysoprase, sard, and sardonyx, without taking account of the imprecise differences in color and banding which underly the Western popular terminology.

55. *Stone of Feng-hua* (Feng-hua-*hsien*, Ming-*chou* [W. Chekiang])
    A coarse-textured yellow stone with marked cleavage, found in the mountains. It bears black stains suggestive of forest scenes and whirling mists. Though it may be worked into palettes and screens, the natives are unaware of its worth.

56. *Stone of Chi-chou* (near Chi-*chou* [Kiangsi])
    A rather coarse purplish stone, excellent for palettes. These are superior to the inkslabs made of Stone of Hua-yen and of Yung-chia. It is also made into square containers and other vessels.

For Stone of Hua-yen, see No. 92 below. Stone of Yung-chia, in Chekiang, is not described in this book.

57. *Stone of Wu-yüan* (Wu-yüan-*hsien*, Hui-*chou* [N.E. Kiangsi])

Several varieties, found in the water, are all used to make palettes. One kind, with starlike markings, is called "Dragon Tail," presumably because it is found in Dragon Tail Torrent. This was much used in former times. It is rather friable: the best variety yields acicular fragments when rubbed with the hand. Some have threadlike patterns, or spots like melon seeds or eyebrows. Another variety is unmarked blue and makes excellent inkslabs. Thick slabs of a violet species found at Ch'i-men-*hsien* are greatly prized, and their price has doubled of late. Still another kind is striated blue; this is found at "Little Ditch" in She-*hsien*. This too is used for palettes, but is not coarse enough to produce much ink, and is not valued locally.

Possibly this is a schist.

58. *Stone of T'ung-yüan* (T'ung-yüan-*chün* [E. Kansu])

The natives strike fishlike water creatures, whose cry is "miek! miek!," with clubs and other hard objects, at which they turn into dark-blue glossy stones, which make fine whetstones.

Tu Wan was not skeptical of village advertising.

59. *Stone of Lu-ho* (Lu-ho-*hsien*, Chen-*chou* [S. Kiangsu])

This white agate, found in a sandy riverbed, is used to make Buddhist images.

In the seventeenth century these pebbles were used to pave garden paths. See O. Sirén, *Gardens*, p. 67.

60. *Stone of Lan-chou* (Yellow River, Lan-*chou* [Kansu])

Pieces in different colors, some banded, are found in the river. Some have the forms of creatures. Among them are yellow-striped pebbles, the matrix of true jade. A very lustrous blue-black kind makes an excellent touchstone for gold. I had a round blue one, the size of a persimmon, which I used as a paperweight. One day, after it had been long in storage in a damp place, it fell and broke into several pieces. There was a central cavity in which was a little fish which jumped about for a moment and died.

The expression *chen yü p'u* 真玉璞 means, judging from other similar occurrences, stone resembling rough pieces of uncut jade, still in the matrix. It would be remarkable if true jade had been found in Kansu in historic times. Touchstones are usually a lustrous, black variety of quartz, called basanite. In the two places where Tu Wan describes touchstones, he has no special name for them; he says simply "they are suitable for testing gold" (*k'o shih chin* 可試金). By the fourteenth century, however, the name "gold-testing stone" (*shih chin shih* 試金石) had come into use. See *Ko ku yao lun*, 7, 149–150. This source notes the presence of such stones in the upper Yangtze; it states that they should be cleaned with salt or walnut oil after use; it observes that a similar stone is used to test grades of silver.

61. *Stone of Tzu-chou* (Tzu[b]-*chou* [Shantung])

A white stone with black, cloud-like blotches. The

natives make various kinds of bowls and dishes of it.

This may well be a limestone stained with manganese oxide. *Shan-tung t'ung chih* (1934 ed., 41, 1520), mentions a similar stone with dendritic patterns ("Pine-branch Stone") in this area. They are doubtless identical. There is unusually wide divergence among the several editions of the text in the name of this locality. Both Liu 溜 and Ho 河 occur, and both are wrong. The correct version is clearly Tzu 淄 , as in *Ming ch'ao pen Shuo fu*, from which Liu 溜 is an easy corruption.

62. *Stone of Ting-chou* (Ch'i-tu Mountain, Ting-*chou* [N. Hunan])
    Hollow, purplish-black stones, with many adhering bits of rock. The interior is filled with yellow earth. These are called "Left-over Rations of T'ai-i" (*T'ai-i yü liang* 太乙餘糧). If the cavity is scraped out, they may be used as water flasks accessory to ink palettes, or as containers for water-grown sweet flags.

These divine stones, important in Taoist medicine, and sometimes known as "Left-over rations of the Great Yü" (*Ta Yü yü liang* 大禹餘糧), are limonite nodules. A photograph of an ancient specimen, preserved among the court drugs of medieval Japan, may be seen as Plate 13B in Asahina Yasuhiko, ed., *Shōsōin yakubutsu* (Osaka, 1955).

63. *Purple Gold Stone* (Purple Gold Mountain, Shou-ch'un-*fu* [Anhwei])
    A purple stone, excellent for palettes. My household possesses an ancient palette of this material, which shows the form of the graph 風 (*feng* "wind").

64. *Stone of Chiang-chou* (Chiang-*chou* [S. Shansi])
A whitish stone with wavy patterning, resembling
cow horn, hence the local name "horn stone." It
is made into palettes, but is better for vermilion
than for black ink.

65. *Stone of Ch'en-chou* (Torrent of the Barbarians,
Ch'en^a-*chou* [W. Hunan])
The aborigines employ this black stone, which
they find in the river, to grind their knives. It is
called "black stone" because it colors the water
black. A variety rather like that of Chieh-*chou* is
cut into utensils and seals. A coarser kind makes
palettes, but the smooth is more rare.

66. *Arrow Barb Stones* (White Sheep Horn, atop the
Empyrean Scandent Pass, near Hsin-kan-*hsien*,
Lin-chiang-*chün* [Kiangsi])
Stone arrowheads, three or four inches long, and
still sharp, are found about the foundations of
ancient fortifications. Some are small, and these
are what Confucius called "Arrows of *hu*-wood
(楛) with barbs of stone," which are products
of the Su-shen people, and are also referred to in
"The Tribute of Yü" as from Ching-*chou* and
Liang-*chou*. They are therefore of immense antiquity. Here also are "stone armor-leaves" (*shih
chia yeh*   石甲葉   ), shaped like the carapaces
of tortoises, and stone axheads with holes where
the hafts were. All these are of hard blue stone.

The statement attributed to Confucius is in *Kuo yü* (Lu yü);
it tells of the gift of these arrows to Wu Wang when he was

campaigning against the Shang state. The Su-shen people were settled in Southern Manchuria, and are known under various names down into historic times. Arrowheads of this manufacture were prized as royal treasures in late Chou. (See Laufer, *Jade*, pp. 57–58.) The site of these finds is not easily identified. *YTCS*, 34, 6b–7a, lists a "White Sheep Pass" northeast of Hsin-kan and a "Sheep Horn Pass" southeast of Hsin-kan, but has no "Empyrean Scandent Pass." *Ming i t'ung chih*, 55, 2b, has a "Empyrean Scandent Peak" on Ko-tsao Mountain near here.

67. *Stone of Shang-yu* (Shang-yu-*hsien*, Ch'u-*chou* [S. Chekiang])

    Rather coarse stone, purplish or gray, maculated with green nimbi. It is used for water pots and for balustrades, and connoisseurs make flagstones of it, resembling the pattern of tortoise shell when set in the earth.

68. *Snail Stones* (Chiang-ning-*fu* [S. Kiangsu])

    Banded agate pebbles found in the river, similar to those of Lu-ho-*hsien* and other places. They are admirably translucent.

LOWER SCROLL

69. *Thuja Agate Stone* (Huang-lung-*fu* [Manchuria])

    A white agate showing what appear to be thuja branches in black or yellow, hence the name. Po Meng-heng was envoy to the Northern Caitiffs not long ago, and their chieftain gave him a specimen the size of a peach, bearing the image of a mynah the size of a bean, perched in a thuja branch. There is also an opaque kind with a central hollow. I possess one of these, the largeness of a jujube, in which I keep pills.

The stone is moss agate. Po Meng-heng is the minister Po Shih-chung, a contemporary of Tu Wan. His biography (*Sung shih*, 371, 5455a) says nothing of the mission referred to here. The caitiffs are the Jurchen. Shih-chung was degraded as unfit for office after these barbarians took Kaifeng in 1126.

70. *Precious Flower Stone* (T'ien-t'ai-*hsien*, T'ai[b]-*chou* [Chekiang])

A mottled white stone, like that of Lai-*chou*. Though made into cooking pots and other vessels, it does not hold up well on the fire.

71. *Stone of Shih-chou* [W. Shansi])

A soft, translucent stone, blue-violet or pale yellow, which resembles the steatite of Kuei[a]-*chou*. It is carved into Buddhist images and other objects of great delicacy. It also makes lithographic stamps (*t'u hua yin chi* 圖畫印記) which impress words and pictures most exquisitely.

Probably an alabaster (gypsum).

72. *Stone of Kung* (Kung-*chou* [Kansu])

A glossy, veined green stone, named "Waves on Water." The mine collapsed long ago, so that no more is available. My father gave a round one to Su Tung-p'o, who called it "Sky Waves."

73. *Stone of Yen Mountains* (*Yen Mountains* [N. Hopei])

A white, translucent, lustrous stone, found in the water. It is called "Abducted Jade" (*to yü*

奪玉　　), and resembles true jade. It is made into utensils and other things locally.

The description suggests chalcedony.

74. *Stone of Shao* (Shao-*chou* [N. Kwangtung])
     Occurs in several shades of green, of which the deepest is carved into utensils. One variety shows blue and green bandings, which sometimes resemble mountains. An arenaceous kind, if clarified by boiling and ground to powder, is used as a pigment. This material is created by cupreous vapors. Malachite, some mixed with azerite.

75. *Peach Flower Stone* (Shao-*chou* [N. Kwangtung])
     Mottled pink and white, shaped into vessels or paperweights.

"Peach Flower Stone" from other parts of China is described by the pharmacologists as being a very soft material. They say it will not adhere to the tongue, which means that it resembles clay without being unctuous. Maybe a form of talc or pyrophyllite is meant. Indeed, Read and Pak, *Compendium*, p. 44, say that a Korean sample proved to be soapstone. K'ou Tsung-shih describes a form with white "flowers" on a pink background. These are presumably rosettes of crystals, like the "Chrysanthemum Stone" illustrated in H. T. Chang, *Lapidarium*. In one variety of the latter the flowers are composed of calcite crystals, in another, of andalusite crystals. Such formations are common, other notable examples being the rosettes of tourmaline found in the rocks of California, and the famous "Cherry-blossom Stone" (*sakura-ishi*　櫻石　) of Japan. In general Read and Pak take the name "Peach Flower Stone" to stand for a kind of

marble, however. Dolomitic marbles are often pink-colored. See
Pen ts'ao kang mu, 9, for a resumé.

76. *Stone of Tuan* (Holy Goat Ravine, Ax-haft
Mountain, near Tuan-*chou* [Kwangtung])
Of the four areas where this kind of stone is produced, that which gives us "Cliff Stone" (*yen shih*
岩石) is the best. This is in the remote mountains, and must be approached by fishing boat and
then on foot. There are many quarries at these
cliffs. One at "Victorious Dragon Cliff" was
mined for its glossy purple stone during early
T'ang, but is no longer worked, since modern
taste prefers the products of other quarries. Of
these latter, the "Mynah Eye" (*ch'ü-yü yen*
鴝鵒眼) from "Lower Cliff" is the most admired, but that mine is exhausted. In its stead we
get "Sparrow Eye" (*ch'üeh-erh yen* 雀兒眼) and
"Grackle Eye" (*liao-ko yen* 了哥眼) from the
nearby "Flanking Cliffs." The "Upper Cliff" is
also quarried for orbicular varieties: its upper pit
produces "Parakeet Eye" (*ying-ko yen* 鸚哥眼)
and its lower pit is worked for "Chicken Neck-
feather Cat Eye" (*chi weng mao-erh yen*
雞翁猫兒眼). The "eyes" are in various
colors, usually surrounded by concentric circles of
different hue. Many of the pits are difficult to
work because of seepage.

"Holy Sheep," for which the ravine is named, is also *ling
yang* 羚羊 , either the serow (*Capricornis* sp.) or the goral
(*Naemorhaedus* sp.), animals related to the chamois and the
American "mountain goat." The ravine was named for a rock supposed to be a petrified goral (*YTCS*, 96, 5b). The identifications
of "parakeet" and "grackle" come from B. Read, "Chinese

Materia Medica VI. Avian Drugs," *Bulletin*, Peking Society of Natural History, 6.4 (June, 1932), 1–112. The stones of the other three areas, similar to the "Cliff Stones," are described under "Stone of Hsiao Hsiang" in the next article. Stone of Tuan-*chou* is the most celebrated of all palette materials. For further information the interested reader is referred to William Hung, "The Inkslab in Chinese Literary Tradition," *Occasional Papers* . . . in Chinese Studies at Yenching University, No. 3 (1940), and to R. H. van Gulik, *Mi Fu on Ink-stones* (Peking, 1938). A fairly detailed contemporary study of the mines and their products is the anonymous *Tuan ch'i yen p'u*, preserved in the great Sung collectanea *Po ch'uan hsiieh hai*. Chao Hsi-hu (fl. 1240), *Tung t'ien ch'ing lu* treats of the same subject, and also discusses eight types of landscape stones. For a good history of the development of the quarries, written early in the nineteenth century, see Wu Lan-hsiu, *Tuan ch'i yen shih*. The oldest reference to this stone known to van Gulik is the notice in *Sung shih*, 5, 4505a, which refers to the termination of local tribute in Tuan stone as of May 17, 991. However, as Hung points out, the material is mentioned in T'ang literature; on this point see also Wu Tseng, *Neng-kai chai man lu* (twelfth century; TSCC ed.), 1, 12. A T'ang example is Liu Yü-hsi's poem "Presented with a Purple Stone Palette of Tuan-*chou*" (*Liu Meng-te wen chi* [SPTK, chap. 4]). Hung points out that inkslabs of stone from She-*chou* (i.e., Stone of Wu-yüan, above) were preferred in the tenth and eleventh centuries, to be replaced in popular affection by those of stone from Tuan-*chou* thereafter. The stone itself, which occurs in various light colors, is apparently a fossiliferous Triassic limestone.

77. *Stone of Hsiao-Hsiang* (W. of Tuan-*chou* [Kwang-tung])

Three other localities near Tuan-*chou* produce palette stone: Hsiao-Hsiang, Hou-li, and "Oyster Mine." All types here are some shade of purple, and orbicular, though the eyes usually lack the haloes of the best material from the "Cliffs." Useful material makes up only a small part of the matrix in which it is enclosed. None of this fetches the prices of the stone from the Cliff Mines, the cheapest of which (from the Flanking Cliffs) costs ten times that of Hsiao-Hsiang.

Hou-li, properly written 後灑 , not 後歷 , is the name of a river. So also, doubtless is Hsiao-Hsiang ("The Little Hsiang"). These three localities are all mentioned in the preceding article, which discusses only the superior stone from the nearby cliffs.

78. *Stone of the Office of the White Horse* (Ho-nan-*fu* [Honan])
    Pieces of stone, in shades of green or blue, washed from the fields by rainstorms. One blue-green (*kan lü* 紺綠) variety resembles the "Beads Worth Horses" (*ma chia chu* 馬價珠) of the Western Barbarians (*hsi fan* 西蕃). Some translucent, plum-sized ones are made into Buddha images. The deep green kind is the most expensive. This stone, produced in foreign countries, is now found on the site of ancient Loyang! Bronze belt hooks, inlaid with various precious stones, are also found here.

"Beads Worth Horses" are the precious beads of the Tibetans, which were not, as has been supposed, turquoises. These became popular only much later. They may have been sapphires, as H. T. Chang has suggested, or possibly emeralds. In the tenth century these expensive gems were said to be *sê-sê*, a term used in T'ang for deep blue and blue-green gem stones, especially lapis lazuli, but later extended to stones of similar habit. What the fragments unearthed at Loyang may have been is a mystery.

There are, unfortunately, many blue and green minerals: soda-lite, prehnite, and lapis lazuli, for instance. It seems that we have here the accidental uncovering of an old lapidary factory, or else a forgotten treasury. Blue and green gem stones of all kinds were treasured in Chinese antiquity. "Office of the White Horse" refers to the supposed site of the famous repository of the first Buddhist texts brought to China under official auspices.

79. *Stone of Mi* (An-ch'iu-*hsien*, Mi-*chou* [Honan])
    A finely streaked white or bluish agate, in a rough matrix, found in the earth and at the water's edge. Formerly it was little valued, and even used by the villagers to build walls. Recently, because of the demand by mandarins, the price has risen astro-nomically.

80. *Stone of Square Mountain* (Square Mountain, Huang-yen-*hsien*, T'ai^b-*chou* [Chekiang])
    Coarse rectangular stones in various colors.

81. *Parrot Stone* (Ching-nan-*fu* [Hupeh])
    Large separate slabs of soft pale green stone. It is ground on a bronze plate and made into utensils.

Part of this article is corrupt and unintelligible, and I may have misunderstood the reference to the bronze plate (*t'ung p'an* 銅盤). The name "parrot stone" is not explained. Some editions also add a line about a fine-grained purple variety suitable for inkstones. This proves to be identical with the final sentence of No. 103 "Stone of Fang-ch'eng," which has been transferred here by mistake.

82. *Pink Thread Stone* (I-tu[b]-*hsien*, Ch'ing-*chou* [Shan-tung])

A rather soft orange-colored stone, with thready striations. It makes a good palette, but is so porous that it must be soaked with water before use. T'ang Lin-fu (also called Yen-yu) classed this among those of highest quality in his catalogue of palettes.

Yen-yu is the courtesy name of T'ang Hsün, who lived during the first half of the eleventh century. He wrote a "Register of Palettes" in three chapters. The name Lin-fu is not recorded in his biography in *Sung shih*, 303, 5304a–b.

83. *Stone Green* (Ch'ien-shan-*hsien*, Hsin-*chou* [E. Kiangsi])

A striated, translucent, lustrous green stone, some-times in the form of connected mountains, used to make utensils. A pale green fragmented sort is boiled and ground to make a cosmetic.

The term *chuang shih* 裝飾 is used of cosmetic prepa-rations in this period, not of decoration generally. Thus all the articles under that rubric in the tenth-century book *Ch'ing i lu* have to do with ladies' makeup. The malachite of the present article was probably used for eye shadow. The mountain also produced both copper (associated with the malachite) and lead (hence its name) from early times. See *YTCS*, 21, 3b-4a.

84. *Stone of Wu-wei* (Wu-wei-*chün* [S. C. Anhwei])

A patterned gray or pale-violet stone bearing images of thuja branches, or of mountains and forests, as if painted in ink. It also comes shaped like Buddhist figurines. It is cut locally into screen slabs.

85. *Stone of Szu-chou* (Chu-tun-chʜn, Szu-chou [N. Kiangsu])
     Pale blue-white chalcedony pebbles, with a crust of sandy matter, found in the sand. The natives make various objects of it.

Here *ma-nao* stands for an unstriated (*wu shua szu* 無刷絲) average chalcedony, rather than an agate.

86. *Arsenical Stone* (——)
     Yü-stone (礜石) is gray-white, and some- times egg-shaped. Storks raise edible fish in ponds by their nests and feed them with this stone. If you try to take some, the storks swallow it and fly away. Recently a man tried to steal some from a stork's nest at a Buddhist monastery in Jui-an- *hsien*, Wen-*chou*; he was caught and interrogated, and claimed that the stones bring good luck. It is also said that the storks use them to warm their eggs.

The earliest example of the stork legend I can find is in Chang Hua's glosses on the *Ch'in ching* (ed. of *Po ch'uan hsüeh hai*, p. 12a). These were done in the third century. Chang Hua attributes the story to the Taoists. The expression *yü*-stone usually refers to an arsenical mineral, though it is uncertain which is meant. Kimura Kōichi, *Wa Kan yakumei mokuroku* (Tokyo, 1946), p. 217, says that it is arsenolite (oxide of arsenic), but the *Kokuyaku honzō kōmoku* makes it arsenopy- rite (sulphide of arsenic and iron). Read and Pak, *Compen- dium*, agrees with Kimura. But the *Yü-shih* of the stork fantasy seems to have nothing to do with arsenic; some other stone must have been called by this name in antiquity. Among various possibilities is an error for *fan shih* 礬石 "alum stone."

87. *Stone of Chin-hua* (Gold Flower Mountain, Wu-chou [Chekiang])

A large stone shaped like a crouching sheep which I myself saw at a Buddhist temple. It is exactly as described in the tradition about Huang Ch'u-p'ing shouting at the stones.

This tale, which appears in *Shen hsien chuan*, tells how Huang Ch'u-p'ing and his brother, shepherds on Chin-hua (Gold Flower) Mountain, had their sheep turned to stone by a Taoist. They became sheep again when Ch'u-p'ing shouted at them. Apparently the one seen by Tu Wan was somehow overlooked.

88. *Stone of Sung-tzu* (Sung-tzu-*hsien*, Ching-nan-*fu* [Hupeh])

Multicolored agates found in the river, similar to those of Chen-*chou*. The natives do not value them.

The Chen-*chou* agates are the Stones of Lu-ho; see No. 59.

89. *Bodhisattva Stone* (Mount O-mei, Chia-*chou* [S. Szechwan])

Translucent stones which show a play of colors when the sun strikes them, found in mountain caverns like those of Mount Wu-t'ai. They are hexagonal, and range in size from that of a jujube to that of a cherry seed.

This famed mineral, also called "Stone which Releases Light" (*fang kuang shih* 放光石), was found in a cave at the "Cliff of the Seven Jewels" on Mt. Omei (*YTCS*, 146, 13a). Tu Wan's description follows closely the language of his contemporary K'ou Tsung-shih (*Pen ts'ao yen i*, A. D. 1116). He omits Tsung-shih's comparison of the stone to rock crystal, as well as the pharmacologist's explanation of the name "Bodhisattva Stone," namely: the adamantine polychrome play made by the passage of light suggests the halo about the head of a Buddha. Li Shih-chen considers it a quartz mineral, and adds that it is used by the alchemists to make "Cases of the Five Metals and the Three Yellows" (*wu chin san huang k'uei* 五金三黃匱). The "Three Yellows" are, according to *Pao p'u tzu*, realgar ("male yellow"), orpiment ("female yellow"), and gold ("yellow metal"). Possibly some kind of artificial gems or inlays are referred to. Several authorities have taken Bodhisattva Stone to be aventurine quartz, that is, crystalline quartz spangled with flakes of mica, etc., an identification apparently first proposed by Abel-Rémusat. Certainly some form of quartz crystal seems likely. *B'uo-sât 菩薩 Stone has sometimes been confused with *Buâ-sâ 婆娑 Stone, a mysterious stone imported from Southern Asia. (For this whole problem, see Laufer, *Sino-Iranica*, p. 526.)

90. *Stone of Khotan* (Khotan Nation [Turkestan])
     Found in hard earth, this stone is deep indigo, sometimes mottled, veined in white, and brilliantly spotted. The latter kind is styled "Gold Star Stone" (*chin hsing shih* 金星石). A deep green glossy variety is called "Kingfisher [feather]" (*fei-ts'ui* 翡翠). Few specimens are unflawed and valuable. The "Kingfisher" variety is prized above the "Gold-Star."

S. H. Hansford regards this as the first reference to the famous jade quarries of Khotan. (See *Chinese Jade Carving* [London,

1950], p. 38.) Elsewhere (in his "Jade and the Kingfisher," *Oriental Art*, 1 [1948], 15) he notes that the term *fei-ts'ui* seems to apply to lapis-lazuli, as in *Ming i t'ung chih*, 89, 14, which notes the presence of a stone of that name in Herat, where lapis is important. Despite this, Hansford prefers to think that during Sung *fei-ts'ui* was a name for dark-green nephrite. His article "Jade and the Kingfisher" gives an interesting account of the history of this term as applied to stones. It is, of course, well known that it has referred to Burmese jadeite since the eighteenth century. But the "Gold Star Stone" here is certainly lapis-lazuli, speckled with bits of golden pyrite, though some minerals classified under this name in the pharmacopoeias are apparently micas, such as phlogopite. Hansford thinks this must have been imported to Khotan from Afghanistan, presumably from the great mines of Badakhshan. In my opinion, since Tu Wan treats "Gold Star Stone" and "Kingfisher Stone" as color varieties of the same substance, and in view of the lapis-lazuli called "Kingfisher" from Herat, *both* are lapis-lazuli. This gemstone was certainly known to the medieval Chinese, as proved by the presence of a cowskin belt set with plaques of lapis-lazuli in the Shōsōin (it is labeled *kan yü tai* 紺玉帶). See Ishida Mosaku and Wada Gun'ichi, *Shōsōin* (Tokyo, Osaka, and Moji, 1954), p. 117.

91.   *Stone of Huang-chou* (Huang-chou [E. Hupeh])
       Translucent pebbles, banded in various colors, found in the river opposite the Red Wall at Wu-ch'ang. Sometimes it has the natural shape of a Buddha; sometimes it is in broken fragments. Su Tung-p'o obtained more than a hundred from a small boy by trading cakes for them. He gave these as a gift to Fo-yin. Consequently, they were much in demand among the aristocracy.

This "Red Wall" is not the one made famous by Su Tung-p'o, though it is not many miles from it. The source of the stones was the Mountain of Assembled Jewels, above the Wall (*YTCS*, 49, 8a). The story of the cakes was narrated by the poet himself in his *Ch'ien Kuai shih kung* (in *Ching chin Tung-p'o wen chi shih lüeh*, 60, 2a-b). He tells where the stones were found, and describes their appearance: ". . . handsome stones, not to be distinguished from jade, abounding in the colors pink, yellow, and white, their patterns like the volutes on a man's finger, attractively delicate and luminous." One day he found a boy bathing in the Ch'i-an River. The lad had been collecting the stones, and Tung-p'o made a game of trading cakes for them, until he had obtained two hundred and ninety-eight. One of them, resembling the head of a tiger or leopard, he designated "Elder of the Horde of Stones." He arranged the collection in an old copper basin, and poured water over them to make them glisten. This display he presented to the merry monk Fo-yin, his boon companion. The latter, a Zen adept, humorously allegorized the nothingness of all things in the world by pouring ink over the stones. This led to a monkish custom, for which Su Tung-p'o takes credit, of making a gift of water poured over stones when the donor could not afford a more expensive one. This episode took place in A. D. 1082. The poet also wrote of a farcical colloquy with Fo-yin after the presentation of the gift (*Hou kuai shih kung*). Fo-yin, also named Liao-yüan, has a biography in *Hsü chuan teng lu*, chap. 5 (*Taishō Tripitaka*, 51, 497–498). The pretty stones seem to have been agates.

92. *Stone of Hua-yen* (Hua-yen River, Wen-chou [S. Chekiang])
    A yellow stone, sometimes spotted with black, used to make vessels. A purple variety makes a fair ink-stone.

Mi Fu describes other color varieties of this stone. He says it produces a fine shiny ink, like lacquer.

93. *Stone of Chien-chou* (Chien[b]-*chou* [Fukien])
A hard, deep purple, maculated stone, used for palettes. It is sometimes sold as the "Mynah Eye" stone of Tuan-*chou*.

94. *Stone of Ju-chou* (Ju-*chou* [Honan])
Large agates, blue, white, or pink, occasionally banded, found in sand and water. These are made into covered dishes, wine vessels, and the like. They have been used only during the past ten years or so.

Possibly these are the "Flowered Stones of Ju" (*hua ju shih* 花汝石) of *Ho-nan t'ung chih* (1914 reprint), 29, 7a.

95. *Bell Teat Stone* (Kuang[a]-*chou*, Lien-*chou*, Li-*chou*, Ch'en[b]-*chou* [Kwangtung and Hunan])
Stones in the forms of tortoises, snakes, toads, crabs, geckos, and various fruits, some in natural colors. I have often collected them. These have doubtless been petrified after prolonged contact with the stone, like the crabs which are swept into the caves on the tide.

Limestone stalactites are called "bell teats" (*chung ju* 鐘乳) from their resemblance to the bosses on bronze bells. (Cf. No 113.)

96. *Rice Stones* (Tung-yang-*hsien*, Wu-*chou* [Chekiang])
Translucent pebbles in many colors, found near a Buddhist temple called "Office of the Paired

Groves." They are made into beads, and sometimes paperweights.

The name *fan shih*   飯石   is unexplained. It has nothing to do with the *mo fan shih*   麥飯石   of the pharmacopoeias, regarded by Read and Pak (*Compendium*, p. 66) as porphyry. *Chia t'ai K'uai-chi chih* (quoted in *Che-chiang t'ung-chih* [1934 ed.], 106, 1887) says that it is amethystine (*tzu shih ying*   紫石英   ). Certainly it is a quartz mineral of some kind. No doubt the beads into which it was made were used on the rosaries of the monks at the nearby temple. Quartz was much used for this purpose in medieval China; see for instance the monk Ennin's reference to rosaries of rock crystal in E. O. Reischauer, *Ennin's Diary* (New York, 1955).

97. *Carbon Stone* (Mountains of Western Shu [Szechwan])
    A very soft, glossy, deep black, stony material, called "carbon jade" (*mo yü*   墨玉   ), found deep in the earth. It is cut into belt hooks and other useful things.

Undoubtedly jet, as suggested in Hansford, *Chinese Jade Carving*, p. 49.

98. *Stone of Nan-chien* (Black and Mild Torrent, Nan-chien-chou [Fukien])
    A lustrous, blue-black stone, taken from the river, which makes good palettes. The natives also make incense braziers and other finely carved utensils of it. It was the stone of Su Tung-p'o's "Phoenix Bill Palette."

The name "Phoenix Bill Stone" (*feng chou shih* 鳳味石)
was originally given by Su Tung-p'o to a hill in the shape
of a drinking phoenix, near the great tea plantations of
the Northern Park (*po yüan* 北苑) at Chien-*chou*. The
bird's bill seemed to approach a stone, and it was the latter
which was cut into these palettes. Later the name was transferred to this palette material from Nan-chien-*chou*, south of
Chien-*ehou*. (See *Tung-p'o ch'i-chi*, 1, 20, and *YTCS*, 133, 6b.)

99. *Stone Mirror* (Wu Torrent, Ch'i-yang-*hsien*, Yung-
     chou [S. Hunan])
     A splendent blue-black stone, several feet broad,
     standing by the mountainside. It reflects objects
     from a considerable distance, hence the name.
     There is another such reflecting stone at Lin-an-
     hsien in Hang-*chou*.

A certain Liu Yüan wrote of this stone in his "Preface to the
Stone Speculum" (*shih chien hsü*   石鑑序   ), in which he
states that it must first be rinsed with water to make it reflect
properly. (See *YTCS*, 56, 5b.) Such natural mirrors are not uncommon. They seem to have provoked some disquiet in ob-
servers, to judge from the example of the stone mirror at Chi-
nan, within whose shining surface bogles lurked (see *Yu-yang
tsa tsu* [*SPTK* ed.], 10, 3b).

100. *Lang-kan Stone* (Ch'ang-kuo-*hsien*, Ming-*chou*
     [Chekiang])
     A coral-like stone found in shallow water along
     the coast. Some specimens are two or three feet
     high. They must be pulled up by ropes let down
     from rafts. Though white when first taken from
     the water, they turn a dull purple after a while.
     They are patterned everywhere with circles, like

ginger branches, and are rather brittle. Though the natives hold them in little regard, they are sometimes used in the construction of artificial mountains in the far Northwest.

Lang-kan　琅玕　is mentioned in the oldest Chinese books, including *Shu ching, Shan hai ching* and *Erh ya*, to name only a few. In these sources it is always ascribed to the far Northwest, especially the mysterious Mountains of K'un-lun. It is sometimes described as a stone, sometimes as a gem ("jade"), or a bead ("pearl"), or a tree. The problem of finding an identification in this welter of apparent contradictions has attracted the labor of H. T. Chang (*Lapidarium*, pp. 23–30). He concludes that the red *lang-kan* of antiquity, beadlike, or the fruit of fairy trees, is ruby spinel ("Balas") from Badakhshan, whereas the blue *lang-kan* of later times, frequently mentioned in T'ang and Sung sources, is a species of coral, though he takes examples attributed to the West in this age to be turquoise. Read and Pak (*Compendium*, p. 21) call it malachite. Certainly the *lang-kan* of the Chekiang coast is a kind of native coral. Indeed, I think that *all lang-kan* was coral. The red beads of antiquity, which grew on trees, must have been the precious red coral of the Mediterranean, imported through Central Asia to China. Chavannes long ago identified the *lang-kan* of Ta Ch'in as coral (*T'oung pao*, 8 [1907], 182), and Li Shih-chen wrote in the sixteenth century: "men of antiquity called the prasine kind [of *shan-hu*] 'blue-green *lang-kan*'; it too is adaptable to the making of beads." (*Pen ts'ao kang mu*, 8.) In short, *shan-hu* and *lang-kan* are virtual synonyms, perhaps ancient loan-words for "coral" from different places, perhaps Chinese dialect words, or perhaps names for two color varieties. The artificial mountains manufactured in the Northwest are a puzzle. One is reminded of the "Mountains of Prasine *Kan*" (*pi kan shan*　碧玕山　), one of them decorated in gold, which were sent more than once as "tribute" to the Sung court by the Thais of Ta-li (*Sung shih*, 488, 5714a). These could have been made of malachite or of green turquoise, but coral is equally a possibility.

101. *Cabbage Leaf Stone* (Han-*chou-chün* [Szechwan])
"Cabbage Leaf Jade Stone" (*ts'ai yeh yü shih*
菜葉玉石) is a hard translucent stone, whose
color ranges from pale blue to indigo. After
quarrying, the native workmen saw it into thin
pieces with iron blades, to which sand and water
have been applied. These slices become "echo
slabs" (*hsiang pan* 響板) and heavy foot
rules (*chieh fang ya ch'ih* 界方壓尺). The
stone is also made into other utensils.

"Echo slabs" are gongs that echo the sound of the human
voice; they are sometimes called "echo stones." The foot rules
were also used as paperweights.

102. *Stone of Ts'ang-chou* (Ts'ang-chou [E. Hopei])
A soft, brittle, white stone, found in the sand on
the seashore. It is known as "Webbed Thread
Stone" (*lo szu shih* 絡絲石) because of its
reticulated surface. Suitable pieces are cemented
together to make simulated mountains.

103. *Stone of Fang-ch'eng* (Fang-ch'eng-*hsien*, T'ang-
chou [Honan])
A rather soft, pale green, glossy stone; also deep
purple or gray. It makes various utensils. The
purple kind is excellent for palettes.

104. *Stone of Teng-chou* (Sha-men and other small
islands off Teng-*chou* [Shantung])
Black and white stones, of which *go* (*ch'i* 棋)
"men" are manufactured. There are also beautiful

pebbles in many colors at the base of the sea cliffs, some as if patterned in gold. A gentleman of the eleventh century made a collection of these, and took them to Canton by ship, where they were praised by Su Tung-p'o.

105. *Stone of Yü-shan* (Yü-shan-*hsien*, Hsin-*chou* [E. Kiangsi])
A bluish stone, found in a stream near Pin-hsien Hamlet, which is used to make palettes. Palettes of new design sold recently there are shaped like lotus and apricot leaves.

A favorite form for dishes and other shallow containers. Compare the leaf-shaped agate dish in the Shōsōin (Ishida and Wada, *Shōsōin*, fig. 62.)

106. *Snowy Wave Stone* (Chung-shan-*fu* [W. Hopei])
A dark-gray stone with meandering crisscross white veins. Su Tung-p'o took a specimen home with him and named it "Snowy Wave Stone" (*hsüeh lang shih* 雪浪石).

See Su's poem in *Tung-p'o*, 8, 26b. The title of the poem in this edition has *yün* 雲 "cloud" for *hsüeh* 雪 "snow," but the latter character appears in the poem itself.

107. *Stone of Hang* (Hang-*chou* [Chekiang])
White translucent crystals, some sharply pointed like cinnabar. They are put together into small facsimile mountains.

Quartz? Calcite?

108. *Stone of the Great T'o* (Kuei[b]-*chou* [W. Hupeh])
A blue-black river stone, maculated like a francolin,
rather coarse, and suitable for palettes. The natives
of these gorges call the Chiang River the T'o
(沱), hence the name of the stone.

The T'o is, of course, a section of the upper Yangtze. This
palette material was admired by Tu Fu and by Ou-yang Hsiu.
See *YTCS*, 74, 5a. The stones form a unique glacial deposit of
Cambrian age. See Chang, *Lapidarium*, pp. 243–244.

109. *Stone of Ch'ing-chou* (Ch'ing-*chou* [Shantung])
A purplish stone, mined to make inkstones of inferior quality, though they are much used in the
vicinity.

Wm. Hung, "Inkslab," p. 13, says that this is a red-brown
limestone; it was requarried for the same purpose by the Japanese in 1922. It should be noted that although I have translated
tzu 紫 by "purple" throughout, the word also covers some dull
reds.

110. *Dragon Fang Stones* (Ning-hsiang-*hsien*, T'an-*chou*
[Hunan])
This purple stone, called "dragon fang" (*lung ya*
龍牙) occurs as water boulders or is quarried
in the mountains, and is converted into palettes.

111. *Stone* Go "Men" (O-*chou* [E. Hupeh])
These round, flat pebbles, both black and white,
are natural *go*-counters. They are found in the
water at a place called "Stone Casket Head" (*shih*

k'uei t'ou   石匱頭   ). The black ones will also serve as touchstones. An old crone who lives in the mountains makes a living selling them. Traditionally the stones were a gift of the gods to her.

Apparently these are quartz pebbles, milky quartz and glossy black basanite. Cf. No. 104.

112. *Stone of Fen-i* (Fen-i-*hsien*, Yüan-*chou* [W. Kiangsi])
Glossy, purple, water-borne stones, about six or seven inches in diameter. They are used to make palettes, but need considerable polishing because of their rough surface. They are quite uncommon.

113. *Bell Teat Stone* (Chin-hua-*hsien*, Wu-*chou* [Chekiang])
In the "Three Grottoes of the Wise Ones" (*chih che san tung*   智者三洞   ) there are stony slopes like snowbanks. Here I found a small piece shaped like two dragons with intertwined tails. They had doubtless been petrified when tinctured by the stalactite stone. This specimen had several holes in it, in which I planted sweet flags. Afterwards I gave it to a connoisseur. There is a natural stone drum in the cave, which sounds when struck.

114. *Stone of Fou-kuang* (Fou-kuang Mountain, Kuang[b]-*chou* [S. Honan])
A rather coarse, translucent, white stone, which resembles Stone of Chieh-*chou*. It is cut into vessels and seals.

Possibly a crystalline limestone.

Index of Chinese Names

PERSONS

Asahina Yasuhiko   朝比奈泰彦

Chang Ch'üan-i   張全義
Chang clan   張氏
Chang, H. T.   張鴻釗
Chang Hai-p'eng   張海鵬
Chang Hao   張淏
Chang Hua   張華
Ch'ang Mao   常懋
Chao Hsi-hu   趙希鵠
Ch'eng Ta-ch'ang   程大昌
Chi-yang   李陽
Chia Szu-tao   賈似道
Chiang Ying-shu   蔣穎叔
Ch'ien Sun-shu   錢遜叔
Chou Mi   周密
Chu Chiu-ting   諸九鼎
Chu Hsi   朱熹
Chu Mien   朱勔

Fan Li   范蠡
Fang Shuo   方勺
Fo-yin   佛印

Han Kan   韓幹
Ho Hsien-ku   何仙姑
Ho Tzu-hsiao   何紫霄
Hsiao Pao-chüan   蕭寶卷

Tu Wan	杜綰
Tu Yen	杜衍
Wada Gun'ichi	和田軍一
Wang Chin-ch'ing	王晉卿
Wang K'uo-fu	王郭夫
Wang Tso	王佐
Wei Yang-yü	雌揚俞
Wu Lan-hsiu	吳蘭修
Wu Tseng	吳曾
Yeh Meng-te	葉夢得
Yeh Shao-yün	葉少蘊
Yen-yu	彦猷
Yü Hsing-tsung	于興宗
Yüan Chieh	元結
Yüan Tz'u-shan	元次山
Yün lin chü shih	雲林居士

PLACES*

An-ch'iu	安邱
An-fu	安福
An-yang	安陽
Ancestral Shrine of the White Horse	白馬廟
Apartment of Cloudy Stone Mountain	雲石山房
Ax-haft Mountain	斧柯山
Basilica of Promulgated Accord	宣和殿
Black and Mild Torrent	踏淡溪

---

* Here I omit all administrative designations suffixed to place names, like *chou* 州 , *chün* 軍 , *chen* 鎮 *hsien* 縣 and *fu* 府 . Ch'eng-*chou*, for instance appears here only as Ch'eng. A few homophones, both true and apparent, occur, and these are distinguished by superscript [a] and [b]. Thus Hsiang[a] is 相 and Hsiang[b] is 湘 .

Ch'ang-shan	常山
Chao-hsin	招信
Chen	真
Chen-chiang	鎮江
Chen-yang	鎮陽
Ch'en[a]	辰
Ch'en[b]	郴
Ch'eng	成
Chi	吉
Chi-nan	濟南
Chi-pu River	濟步江
Ch'i-an	崇安
Ch'i-men	祁門
Ch'i-tu	祁闍
Ch'i-yang	祁陽
Chia	嘉
Chiang	絳
Chiang River	江水
Chiang-hua	江華
Chiang-ling	江陵
Chiang-ning	江寧
Chiao-k'ou	交口
Chieh	湝
Chien[a]	簡
Chien[b]	建
Chien-k'ang	建康
Ch'ien-shan	鉛山
Ch'ien-t'ang	錢塘
Chin-hua	金華
Ching	荆
Ching-nan	荆南
Ch'ing	青
Ch'ing-ch'i	清溪
Ch'ing-yün Hamlet	慶雲鄉

Jui-an	瑞安
K'ai-feng	開封
K'ai-hua	開化
Kao-an	高安
Khotan	于闐
Kiosk of the Myriad Stones	萬石亭
Ko-tsao Mountain	閤皁山
Kuan-chung	關中
Kuang^a	廣
Kuang^b	光
Kuang-nan	廣南
Kuei^a	桂
Kuei^b	歸
K'un-shan	崑山
K'un-lun	崑崙
Kung	鞏
Kuo	虢
Lai	萊
Lan	蘭
Le-p'ing	樂平
Lei-yang	耒陽
Li	澧
Liang	梁
Lien	連
Lin-an	臨安
Lin-chiang	臨江
Lin-lü	林慮
Ling-ling	零陵
Ling-pi	靈壁
Lithophone Mountain	磬山
Little Ditch	小溝
Lo River	洛河

T'ien-t'ai	天台
Ting	鼎
Torrent of Szu	思溪
Torrent of the Barbarians	蠻溪
Ts'ang	滄
Tsou	鄒
Tuan	端
Tung-t'ing	洞庭
Tung-yang	東陽
T'ung-yüan	通遠
Turtle Shoal	籠
Tzu[a]	梓
Tzu[b]	淄
Vast Cliff	洪巖
Victorious Dragon Cliff	勝龍巖
Village of Disordered Stones	亂石里
Wan-tsai	萬載
Wen	溫
Western Shu	西蜀
White Sheep Horn	白羊角
Wu	婺
Wu Torrent	浯溪
Wu-ch'ang	武昌
Wu-k'ang	武康
Wu-tu	武都
Wu-wei	無為
Wu-yüan	婺源
Yellow Mountain	黃山
Yellow Ox Shoal	黃牛灘
Yen	兗
Yen Mountains	燕山

Ying	英
Ying-ch'ang	穎昌
Yung	永
Yung-chia	永嘉
Yung-k'ang	永康
Yung-ming	永明
Yung-ning	永寧
Yü-shan	玉山
Yüan	袁
Yüeh-sui	越嶲
Yün	筠
Yün-kang	雲岡

LITERATURE

An-hui t'ung chih	安徽通志
Basic Herbs with Amplified Interpretations	本草衍義
Canon of the Basic Herbs of Shen Nung	神農本草經
Che chiang lu	哲匠錄
Che-chiang t'ung chih	浙江通志
Chi chu fen lei Tung-p'o hsien sheng shih	集注分類東坡先生詩
Chia t'ai K'uai-chi chih	嘉泰會稽志
Ch'ien kuai shih kung	菏怪石供
Chih pu tsu chai ts'ung shu	知不足齋叢書
Chin shu	晉書
Ching chin Tung-p'o wen chi shih lüeh	經進東坡文集事略
Ch'in ching	禽經
Ch'ing i lu	清異錄
Chou yün shih chi	縐雲石記

Chung-kuo ying-tsao hsüeh-she
　　hui-k'an　　　　　　　　　　　中國營造學社彙刊

Ch'ung hsiu cheng ho ching shih
　　cheng lei pen ts'ao　　　　　　重修政和經史證類本草

Ch'ün fang ch'ing wan　　　　　　群芳清玩

Erh ya　　　　　　　　　　　　爾雅

Fan tzu chi jan　　　　　　　　范子計然

Han shu　　　　　　　　　　　漢書

History of Palettes　　　　　　　硯史

Ho-nan t'ung chih　　　　　　　河南通志

Hou kuai shih kung　　　　　　　後怪石供

Hsi ching tsa chi　　　　　　　　西京雜記

Hsi yin hsüan ts'ung shu　　　　惜陰軒叢書

Hsin hsiu pen ts'ao　　　　　　　新修本草

Hsü chuan teng lu　　　　　　　續傳燈錄

Hsüan ho hua p'u　　　　　　　宣和畫譜

Hsüan ho shih p'u　　　　　　　宣和石譜

Hsüan ho shu p'u　　　　　　　宣和書譜

Hsüeh chin t'ao yüan　　　　　　學津討原

Hsüeh hai lei pien　　　　　　　學海類編

Hu-nan t'ung chih　　　　　　　湖南通志

Hu-pei t'ung chih　　　　　　　湖北通志

Hua-yang Kung chi shih　　　　　華陽宮記事

Illustrated Canonical Basic Herbs　圖經本草

K'ai ming　　　　　　　　　　開明

Ken yüeh chi　　　　　　　　　艮嶽記

Kokuyaku honzō kōmoku　　　　國譯本草綱目

Ko ku yao lun　　　　　　　　格古要論

Ku chin shuo hai　　　　　　　古今說海

Ku chin t'u shu chi ch'eng　　　古今圖書集成